BADEN-POWELL'S

SCOUTING
FOR BOYS

Presented to:

Brian Stewart.

On "Going Up" October 1961

Akela.

Gordonstown Wolf Cub Pack.

B. - P.

BADEN-POWELL'S
SCOUTING
for BOYS

BOYS' EDITION

LONDON
C. ARTHUR PEARSON LTD.
TOWER HOUSE, SOUTHAMPTON STREET
STRAND, W.C.2

ISSUED UNDER THE AUTHORITY OF
THE BOY SCOUTS ASSOCIATION

©

BOY SCOUTS ASSOCIATION

BOYS' EDITIONS

First published	. . .	*1932*
Reprinted	. . .	*1934*
Revised Edition	. . .	*1936*
Reprinted	. . .	*1937*
Reprinted	. . .	*1940*
Revised Edition	. . .	*1941*
Revised Edition	. . .	*1944*
Reprinted	. . .	*1944*
Reprinted	. . .	*1945*
Reprinted	. . .	*1945*
Reprinted	. . .	*1946*
Reprinted	. . .	*1946*
Reprinted	. . .	*1947*
Reprinted	. . .	*1947*
Revised Edition	. . .	*1950*
First Abridged Edition	. .	*1953*
Reprinted	. . .	*1954*
Reprinted	. . .	*1956*
Reprinted	. . .	*1957*
Reprinted	. . .	*1958*
Reprinted	. . .	*1959*
Reprinted	. . .	*1960*

PRINTED AND BOUND IN ENGLAND BY
HAZELL WATSON AND VINEY LTD
AYLESBURY AND SLOUGH

INTRODUCTION

THIS book was written for boys like you. B.-P. was one of the most famous of Army Scouts; his most exciting adventures happened in Africa when he had to match his wits against native warriors and trackers; one slip, and they would have caught him and shown no mercy. They called him "Impeesa," which means "the Wolf who does not sleep," because they recognised his courage and skill. Then in one expedition he had to make roads, build bridges over rivers and streams, make bivouacs and organise scouting parties. So you see he knew from experience all about the things he wrote of in this book.

One of his jobs was the training of Scouts in the Army. He discovered that the men thoroughly enjoyed this work and became better men for it. So he thought that boys too should have the fun of being Scouts and the chance of learning how to become more useful to their country. First he tried the idea out at a camp at Brownsea Island in 1907, and found it worked. The boys were of different types and they were thrilled with it all. Of course, they were exceptionally lucky. They had B.-P. himself to teach them tracking and cooking and all the other outdoor things of camp life, and round the camp fire he would yarn to them of his own experiences and adventures.

After that camp he set to work and wrote down for other boys the yarns he told at Brownsea Island—and here they are in this book for you. If I were you, I shouldn't try to read it straight through; take it yarn by yarn and then try to do some of the things suggested. That's what the first boys did when *Scouting for Boys* was published in 1908, for they didn't get it all at once in one book like this; it came out in fortnightly parts, so they had to read it by instalments. Very soon several boys would get together and become a Patrol, and, without much help, they trained themselves as Boy Scouts.

Things are different now; there are Boy Scout Troops everywhere, and I am sure that after reading these pages you will want to join a Troop. If you have any difficulty in finding a Troop just write to The Boy Scouts Association, Imperial Headquarters, 25, Buckingham Palace Road, London, S.W.1, and they will put you in touch with the nearest Scoutmaster.

B.-P. has passed from us; at the end of this book we have printed his last message to his Scouts. Read it carefully and think it over. He tells you what a happy life he had, but he got so much happiness *out* of life by putting a lot of happiness *into* the lives of millions of boys like you; the secret was that he learnt how to be useful to others, and if you become a Boy Scout you will follow in his footsteps.

So, come along and join us. You will get lots of fun; you will become strong and healthy, learn all about outdoor life like a pioneer or backwoodsman, and at the same time you will make yourself a finer man and citizen.

Good Scouting to you!

LORD SOMERS,

Chief Scout 1941–1944.

When our old Chief died he asked that Lord Somers should succeed him because he knew that he was a great leader and a man of great courage. As you know he was not spared to us for very long and perhaps most of you never had a chance to see him, but you can read his "Introduction" to this edition and learn from it how much we lost by his death. I would not change a word of it, for it puts so much better than I could the story of Scouting. I will only echo what he said: "Come along and join us. Good Scouting to you all."

Rowallan.

Chief Scout.

CONTENTS

THE PROMISE

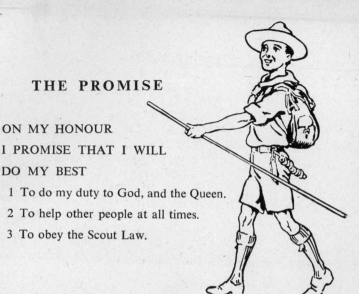

ON MY HONOUR

I PROMISE THAT I WILL

DO MY BEST

  1 To do my duty to God, and the Queen.

  2 To help other people at all times.

  3 To obey the Scout Law.

THE SCOUT LAW

1 A Scout's honour is to be trusted.

2 A Scout is loyal to the Queen, his Country, his Scouters, his Parents, his Employers, and to those under him.

3 A Scout's duty is to be useful, and to help others.

4 A Scout is a friend to all, and a brother to every other Scout, no matter to what country, class or creed the other belongs.

5 A Scout is courteous.

6 A Scout is a friend to animals.

7 A Scout obeys orders of his Parents, Patrol Leader, or Scoutmaster, without question.

8 A Scout smiles and whistles under all difficulties.

9 A Scout is thrifty.

10 A Scout is clean in thought, word and deed.

SCOUTING FOR BOYS

CAMP FIRE YARN. No. 1
SCOUTS' WORK

Peace Scouts

I SUPPOSE every boy wants to help his country in some way or other. There is a way, by which he can do so easily, and that is by becoming a scout.

A scout, as you know, is generally a soldier who is chosen for his cleverness and pluck to go out in front of an army in war to find out where the enemy are, and report to the commander all about them.

But, besides war scouts, there are also peace scouts, i.e. men who in peace time carry out work which requires the same kind of abilities. The trappers of North America, hunters of Central Africa, the pioneers, explorers, and missionaries over Asia and all the wild parts of the world, the bushmen and drovers of Australia, the constabulary of North-West Canada and of South Africa—all are peace scouts, real *men* in every sense of the word, and thoroughly up in scoutcraft, i.e. they understand living out in the jungles, and they can find their way anywhere, are able to read meanings from the smallest signs and foot-tracks; they know how to look after their health when far away from any doctors, are strong and plucky, and ready to face any danger, and always keen to help each other. They are accustomed to take their lives in their hands, and to fling them down without any hesitation if they can help their country by doing so.

1

They give up everything, their personal comforts and desires, in order to get their work done. They do not do all this for their own amusement, but because it is their duty to their Sovereign, their fellow-countrymen, or employers.

It is a grand life, but it cannot suddenly be taken up by any man who thinks he would like it, unless he has prepared himself for it beforehand. Those who succeed best are those who learned scouting while they were still boys.

Scouting also comes in very useful in any kind of life you like to take up, whether it is soldiering or even business life in a city. It is even valuable for a man who goes in for science. And how necessary it is for a doctor or a surgeon to notice a small sign like a scout does, and know its meaning!

So I am going to show you how you can learn scoutcraft for yourself and can put it into practice at home.

It is very easy to learn and very interesting when you get into it. You can best learn by joining the "Boy Scouts."

" Kim "

A good example of what a Boy Scout can do is to be found in Rudyard Kipling's story of "Kim."

"Kim," or, to give him his full name, Kimball O'Hara, was the son of a sergeant of an Irish regiment in India. His father and mother died while he was a child, and he had been left to the care of an aunt who lived in a humble way in India.

His playmates were all natives, so he got to talk their language and to know their ways better than any European. He became great friends with an old wandering priest who was tramping about India, and with whom he travelled all over the north part of that country. At last, one day he chanced to meet his father's old regiment on the line of march, and in visiting the camp he was arrested on suspicion of being a thief. His birth certificate and other papers were found on him, and the regiment, seeing that he had belonged to them, took charge of him, and started to educate him. But whenever he could get away for holidays he dressed himself in Indian clothes, and went again among the natives as one of them.

After a time he became acquainted with a Mr. Lurgan, a dealer in old jewellery and curiosities, who, owing to his knowledge from dealing with natives, was also a member of the Government Intelligence Department.

This man, finding that Kim had such special knowledge of native habits and customs, saw that he would make a useful agent for Government Intelligence work, that is, a kind of detective among the natives. But, first of all, before employing him, he put him to one or two tests to see whether he was sufficiently brave and strong-minded.

As a trial of his strong-mindedness he attempted to mesmerise him, that is to say, he tried to make Kim's thoughts obey what was in his own mind. It is possible for strong-minded men to do this with those of weaker mind. The way he attempted it was by throwing down a jug of water so that it smashed to pieces; he then laid his finger on the boy's neck, and wished him to imagine the jug mended itself again. But do what he would to make his thought reach the boy's brain, he failed; Kim saw the jug was broken, and would not believe it was mended, although at one time he nearly obeyed him, for he saw a kind of vision of the jug being mended but it faded away again.

Most boys would have let their mind and eyes wander, and would not have been able to keep them on the one subject, and so would have easily become mesmerised by the man.

Lurgan, finding him strong-minded and quick at learning, then gave him lessons at noticing small details and remembering them, which is the most important point in the training of a scout—it is a thing that he should learn and be practising every hour of the day wherever he may be. Lurgan began it with Kim by showing him a tray full of precious stones of different kinds—he let him look at it for a minute, and then covered it with a cloth, and asked him to state how many stones and what sorts were there. At first he found he could only remember a few, and could not describe them very accurately, but with a little practice he soon got to remember them all quite well. And so, also, with many other kinds of articles which were shown to him in the same way.

Then Kim travelled about the country a great deal with a fine old Afghan horse-dealer to whom he was much attached, who was also an agent of the Intelligence Department. On one occasion Kim was able to do him a good turn by carrying an important message for him secretly; and another time he saved his life by overhearing some natives planning to murder him when he came along. By pretending to be asleep and then having a nightmare which caused him to remove from his position, Kim got him away from the neighbourhood of the would-be murderers, and was able to give warning to his friend in good time.

At last he was made a member of the Secret Service, and was given a secret sign—namely, a badge to wear round his neck and a certain sentence to say, which, if said in a peculiar way, meant he was one of the service. Scouts generally have secret signs by which they can communicate with each other.

Once when travelling in the train Kim met another member whom he did not know. This was a native, who when he got into the carriage was evidently in a great state of alarm, and was rather badly cut about the head and arms. He explained to the other passengers that he had met with an accident from a cart whilst he was driving to the station, but Kim, like a good scout, noticed the cuts were sharp and not grazes such as you would get by falling from a cart, and so did not believe him. While the man was tying up a bandage over his head, Kim noticed that he was wearing a locket like his own; so Kim let his own be seen. Directly the man saw it he brought into conversation some of the secret words, and Kim answered with the proper ones in reply. So then the stranger got into a corner with Kim and explained to him that he was carrying out some secret-service work, and had been found out and hunted by some of the enemies of the Government who had nearly killed him. They probably knew he was in the train and would therefore telegraph down the line to their friends that he was coming. He wanted to get his message to a certain police officer without being caught by the enemy, but he could not tell how to do it if they were already warned of his coming. Kim thereupon hit upon the idea of disguising him.

In India there are a number of holy beggars who go about the country. They wear next to no clothing and smear themselves with ashes, and paint certain marks on their faces; they are considered very holy, and people always help them with food and money. So Kim made a mixture of flour and wood ashes, which he took from the bowl of a native pipe, and he undressed his friend and smeared these all over him, and finally with the aid of a little paint-box which he carried, he painted the proper marks on the man's forehead. He smeared the man's wounds with flour and ashes, partly so as to heal them, and also so that they did not show, and he brushed his hair down to look wild and shaggy like that of a beggar, and covered it with dust, so that the man's own mother would not have known him. Soon afterwards they got to a big station where on the platform they found the police officer to whom the report was to be made. The imitation beggar pushed up against him and got abused by the officer in English; the beggar replied with a string of native abuse into which he introduced the secret words. The police officer, although he had pretended not to know Hindustani, understood it quite well, and at once recognised from the secret words that this beggar was an agent; and so he pretended to arrest him and marched him off to the police-station where he could talk to him quietly. It was thus done without anyone on the platform knowing that they were in league with each other, or that this native beggar was the escaped Intelligence agent.

Finally, Kim became acquainted with another agent of the department—an educated native or Babu as they are called in India—and was able to give him great assistance in capturing two officers who were acting as spies against the British on the northwest frontier of India.

The Babu pretended to the officers that he was the manager for a local native prince who did not like the English and travelled with them for some time as representative of this prince. In this way he got to know where they kept their secret papers in their baggage. At last he got up trouble between them and a holy priest, whom they struck; this caused great excitement among the natives, who rushed off with the baggage and got lost in the darkness. Kim, who was among the natives, opened the luggage and found the secret papers, which he took out and carried to headquarters.

These and other adventures of Kim are well worth reading, because they show what valuable work a Boy Scout could do for his country if he were sufficiently trained and sufficiently intelligent.

Mafeking Cadets

We had an example of how useful boys can be on active service, when a corps of boys was formed in the defence of Mafeking, 1899–1900.

Mafeking was quite a small ordinary country town out on the open plains of South Africa.

Nobody ever thought of its being attacked by an enemy, any more than you would expect your town (or village) to be attacked —the thing was so improbable.

But it just shows you how you must be prepared for what is *possible,* not only what is *probable* in war : and so too, we ought to be prepared in Britain against being attacked by enemies.

Well, when we found we were to be attacked at Mafeking, we told off our garrison to the points that they were to protect—some 700 trained men, police, and volunteers. And then we armed the townsmen, of whom there were some 300. Some of them were old frontiersmen, and quite equal to the occasion; but many of them, young shopmen, clerks, and others, had never seen a rifle before, and had never tried to learn to drill or to shoot, and so they were hopelessly at sea at first. It is not much fun to have to face an enemy who means to kill you, when you have never learned to shoot.

Altogether, then, we only had about a thousand men all told to defend the place, which contained 600 white women and children and about 7,000 natives, and was about five miles round.

Every man was of value, and as their numbers gradually got less, owing to men getting killed and wounded, the duties of fighting and keeping watch at night got harder for the rest. It was then that Lord Edward Cecil, the chief staff officer, got together the boys in the place and made them into a cadet corps, put them in uniform and drilled them; and a jolly smart and useful lot they were. We had till then used a large number of men for carrying orders and messages and keeping look-out, and acting as orderlies, and so on. These duties were now handed over to the boy cadets, and the men were released to go and strengthen the firing-line.

And the cadets, under their sergeant-major, a boy named Good-

LORD EDWARD CECIL AND BOY MESSENGERS IN MAFEKING

year, did right good work, and well deserved the medals which they got at the end of the war. Many of them rode bicycles, and we were thus able to establish a post by which people could send letters to their friends in the different forts, or about the town, without going out under fire themselves; and we made postage stamps for these letters which had on them a picture of a cadet bicycle orderly.

I said to one of these boys on one occasion, when he came in through rather a heavy fire: "You will get hit one of these days riding about like that when shells are flying." And he replied: "I pedal so quick, sir, they'd never catch me." These boys didn't seem to mind the bullets one bit; they were always ready to carry out orders, though it meant risk to their life every time.

Would any of you do that? If an enemy were firing down this street, and I were to tell one of you to take a message across to a house on the other side, would you do it? I am sure you would. But probably you wouldn't much like doing it.

But you want to prepare yourself for it beforehand. It's just like taking a header into cold water; a fellow who is accustomed to bathing thinks nothing of it; he has practised it over and over again, but ask a fellow to do it who has never practised it, and he will funk it.

So, too, with a boy who has been accustomed to obey orders at once, whether there is risk about it or not; the moment you order him to do a thing on active service, no matter how great the danger is to him he does it, while another chap who has never cared to obey would object, and would then be despised as a coward even by his former friends.

But you need not have a war in order to be useful as a scout. As a peace scout there is lots for you to do any day, wherever you may be.

CAMP FIRE YARN. No. 2

SUMMARY OF SCOUTS' COURSE
OF INSTRUCTION

IF you are over 8 and under 11 join the Wolf Cubs, if over 11 join the Scouts. To become a Scout you should

1. Apply to the Secretary of the nearest Local Association. The address can be obtained from Boy Scouts Association, Imperial Headquarters, 25, Buckingham Palace Road, London, S.W.1.

2. Join a Patrol or Troop raised in your neighbourhood, with the written permission of your parents.

One boy is chosen as Leader to command the Patrol, and is called "Patrol Leader." He selects another boy to be second in command, who is called "Second." Two Patrols together can form a "Troop," under a Scoutmaster.

After training as a Tenderfoot you all take the Scout's promise. that is, On my honour, I promise that I will do my best:

1. To do my duty to God, and the Queen.
2. To help other people at all times.
3. To obey the Scout Law.*

You will learn the secret sign of the Scouts (see page 20), and also the call of your Patrol (see pages 25–29).

Every Patrol is named after some animal, and each Scout in it has to be able to make the cry of that animal in order to communicate with his pals, especially at night. Thus you may be "the Curlews," "the Eagles," or "the Owls" if you like. But don't be a "Monkey Patrol," that is a Patrol that plays games but has no discipline and wins no badges. No Scout may ever use the call of another Patrol. The Scout Law binds you to be loyal, kind, obedient, and cheerful. Most of your work then consists in playing scouting games and practices by which you gain experience as Scouts. When you have learned sufficient to pass these tests you can win the badge of either a First Class or Second Class Scout.

That of the First Class Scout consists of an arrow-head and a scroll with the mottor "BE PREPARED" on it. That of the Second Class Scout is the motto alone. The Scout's badge is the arrow-head, which shows the north on a map or on the compass. It is the badge of the scout in the Army, because he shows the way; so, too, a peace scout shows the way in doing his duty and helping others.

* See pages 17–19.

8

The motto on the First Class Badge is the Scout's motto of

BE PREPARED,

which means that a Scout must always be prepared at any moment to do his duty, and to face danger in order to help his fellow-men.

He must prepare himself by previous thinking out and practising how to act in any accident or emergency so that he is never taken by surprise; he knows exactly what to do when anything unexpected happens. The scroll is turned up at the ends like a Scout's mouth, because he does his duty with a smile and willingly. The knot is to remind the Scout to do a good turn to someone daily.

The following subjects are what you have to know about to pass the test as a Scout:

Woodcraft.—This means knowing all about animals, which is gained by following up their foot-tracks and creeping up to them so that you can watch them in their natural state and learn the different kinds of animals and their various habits. You only shoot them if in want of food, but no Scout wilfully kills an animal for the mere sake of killing, unless it is a harmful creature.

By continually watching animals in their natural state, one gets to like them too well to shoot them.

The whole sport of hunting animals lies in the woodcraft of stalking them, not in the killing.

Woodcraft includes, besides being able to see the tracks and other small signs, the power to read their meaning, such as at what pace the animal was going, whether he was frightened or unsuspicious, and so on. It enables the hunter also to find his way in the jungle or desert; it teaches him which are the best wild fruits, roots, etc., for his own food, or which are favourite foods for animals, and therefore, likely to attract them.

In the same way in scouting in civilised countries you read the tracks of men, horses, bicycles, etc., and find out from these what has been going on; noticing by small signs, such as birds suddenly starting up, that someone is moving near, though you cannot see him.

By noticing the behaviour or dress of people, and putting this and that together, you can sometimes see that they are up to no good and can thus prevent a crime, or you can often tell when they are in distress and need help or sympathy—and you can then do what is one of the chief duties of a Scout, namely, help those in distress in any possible way that you can.

Remember that it is a disgrace to a Scout if, when he is with

other people, they see anything big or little, near or far, high or
low, that he has not already seen for himself.

Campaigning.—Scouts must, of course, be accustomed to living
in the open; they have to know how to put up tents or huts for
themselves; how to lay and light a fire; how to kill, cut up, and
cook their food; how to tie logs together to make bridges and
rafts; how to find their way by night, as well as by day, in a
strange country, and so on.

But very few fellows learn or practise these things when they
are living in civilised places, because they get comfortable houses
and beds to sleep in, their food is prepared and cooked for them,
and when they want to know the way "they ask a policeman."

Well, when these fellows go out overseas, or try to go scouting,
they find themselves helpless duffers.

Chivalry.—In the old days the Knights were the scouts of
Britain, and their rules were very much the same as the Scout Law
which we have now. We are their descendants, and we ought to
keep up their good name and follow in their steps.

They considered that their honour was the most sacred thing to
uphold; they would not do a dishonourable thing, such as telling
a lie or stealing; they would really rather die than do it. They were
always ready to fight and to be killed in upholding their king or
their religion, or their honour. Thousands of them went out to
Palestine (the Holy Land) to maintain the Christian religion
against the Mohammedan Turks.

Each Knight had a small following of a squire and some men-
at-arms, just as our Patrol Leader has his Second and four or five
Scouts.

The Knight's patrol used to stick to him through thick and thin
and all carried out the same idea as their leader—namely,

Their honour was sacred.

They were loyal to God, and their king, and to their country.

They were particularly courteous and polite to all women and
    children, and infirm people.

They were helpful to everybody.

They gave money and food where it was wanted, and saved up
    their money in order to do so.

They taught themselves the use of arms in order to protect their
    religion and their country against enemies.

They kept themselves strong and healthy and active in order to
    be able to do these things well.

You Scouts cannot do better than follow the example of your

forefathers, the Knights, who made the tiny British nation into one of the best and greatest that the world has ever known.

One great point about them was that every day they had to do a good turn to somebody, and that is one of our rules. When you get up in the morning, remember that you have to do a good turn for someone during the day; tie an extra knot in your handkerchief; and when you go to bed at night think to whom you did the good turn.

If you should ever find that you had forgotten to do it, you must do two good turns the next day instead. Remember that by your Scout's Promise you are on *your honour* to do it. But do not think that Scouts need do only one good turn a day. They must do one, but if they can do fifty so much the better.

It only counts as a good turn when you do not accept any reward in return.

Saving Life.—You have all heard of the Victoria Cross—the little bronze cross first given by Queen Victoria to men who specially distinguish themselves in action under the fire of the enemy.

But there is the companion medal to it, and that is the Albert Medal for those who distinguish themselves in saving life in peace time. And there is the Stanhope Medal for civilian gallantry, and the Edward Medal for gallantry in mines, and the Royal Humane Society's medals. Then there is the George Cross, and the George Medal, as well as our Scout's Gallantry medals.

And I think the man who wins these medals, as he does in the sudden appalling accidents which occur in big cities, mines, and factories, in everyday life, is no less a hero than the soldier who rushes into the thick of the fight to rescue a comrade amid all the excitement and glamour of the battle.

Thousands of Scouts have won our medals for life-saving, and I hope many more will do so.

It is certain that very many of you will at one time or another get a chance of winning one if you are prepared to seize the opportunity. That is, you must *be prepared* for it; you should know what to do the moment an accident occurs—and do it then and there.

It is not enough to read about it in a book and think that you know how to do it—but you must actually practise, and practise pretty often, the actual things to be done; such as how to cover your mouth and nose with a wet handkerchief to enable you to breathe in smoke, how to make a rope for escaping from fire,

how to open a manhole to let air into a gassy sewer, how to lift
and carry an insensible person, how to collar, save, and revive
apparently drowned people, and so on.

When you have learnt all these things you will have confidence
in yourself, so that when an accident happens and everybody is in
a state of fluster, not knowing what to do, you will quietly step out
and do the right thing.

Endurance.—To carry out all the duties and work of a Scout
properly a fellow has to be strong, healthy, and active. And he
can make himself so if he takes a little care about it.

It means a lot of exercise, like playing games, running, walking,
cycling and so on.

A Scout has to sleep very much in the open, and a boy who is
accustomed to sleep with his window shut will probably suffer,
like many a tenderfoot has done, by catching cold and rheuma-
tism when he first tries sleeping out. The thing is always to sleep
with your windows open, summer and winter, and you will never
catch cold. Personally I cannot sleep with my window shut or with
blinds down, and when living in the country I always sleep outside the house, summer and winter alike.

A short go of Swedish or Ju-jitsu exercises every morning and
evening is a grand thing for keeping you fit—not so much for
making showy muscle as to work all your internal organs, and to
work up the circulation of the blood in every part of you.

A good rub down daily with a wet rough towel, even if you
cannot get a bath, is what every real Scout takes, and is of the
utmost importance.

Scouts breathe through the nose, not through the mouth; in
this way they don't get thirsty; they don't get out of breath so
quickly; they don't suck into their insides all sorts of microbes or
seeds of disease that are in the air; and they don't snore at night,
and so give themselves away to an enemy.

"Deep breathing" exercises are of great value for developing the
lungs, and for putting fresh air (oxygen) into the blood, provided
that they are carried out in the open air, and are not overdone so
as to injure the heart, etc. For deep breathing the breath must be
taken in slowly and deeply through the nose, not through the
mouth, till it opens out the ribs to the greatest extent, especially at
the back; then, after a time, it should be slowly and steadily
breathed out again without strain. But the best deep breathing
after all is that which comes naturally from plenty of running
exercise.

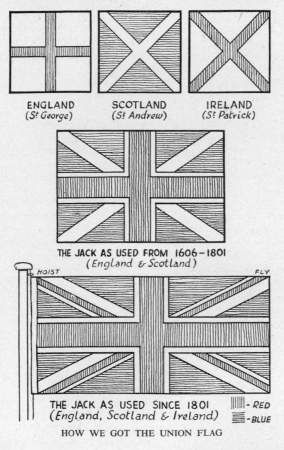

ENGLAND   SCOTLAND   IRELAND
(St George)   (St Andrew)   (St Patrick)

THE JACK AS USED FROM 1606–1801
(England & Scotland)

HOIST   FLY

THE JACK AS USED SINCE 1801   ▨ – RED
(England, Scotland & Ireland)   ▤ – BLUE

HOW WE GOT THE UNION FLAG

Alcohol is now shown to be quite useless as a health-giving drink, and it is mere poison when a man takes much of it. A man who is in the habit of drinking beer, wine or spirits in strong doses every day is not the slightest use for scouting, and very little use for anything else.

Similarly a man who smokes much. The best war scouts don't smoke because it weakens their eyesight; it sometimes makes them shaky and nervous; it spoils their noses for smelling (which is of great importance at night), and the glow of their pipes or even the scent of tobacco carried on them at night, gives them away to watchful enemies. They are not such fools as to smoke. No boy ever began smoking because he liked it, but because he thought it made him look like a grown-up man. As a matter of fact it generally makes him look a little ass.

Patriotism.—Some of you belong to the great British Commonwealth of Nations, one of the greatest that has ever existed in the world.

This vast Commonwealth did not grow of itself out of nothing; it was made by your forefathers by dint of hard work and hard fighting, at the sacrifice of their lives—that is, by their hearty patriotism.

Therefore, in all that you do, remember to think of your country first; don't spend the whole of your time and money on games and tuck shops merely to amuse *yourself,* but think first how you can be of use in helping your country, and, when you have done that, you can justly and honestly sit down and enjoy yourself in your own way. "Country first, self second," should be your motto. Probably, if you ask yourself truly, you will find you have at present got them just the other way about.

If you take up Scouting in that spirit, you will be doing something; take it up, not merely because it amuses you, but because by doing so you will be fitting yourself to help your country. Then you will have in you the true spirit of patriotism, which every British boy ought to have if he is worth his salt.

Winter's Stob ; or, The Elsdon Murder

A brutal murder took place many years ago in the North of England; and the murderer was caught, convicted and hanged chiefly through the scoutcraft of a shepherd boy.

Woodcraft.—The boy, Robert Hindmarsh, had been up on the moor tending his sheep, and was finding his way home over a wild out-of-the-way part of the hills, when he passed a tramp sitting on the ground with his legs stretched out in front of him eating some food.

Observation.—The boy in passing noticed his appearance, and especially the peculiar nails in the soles of his boots.

Concealment.—He did not stop and stare, but just took these things in at a glance as he went by without attracting much attention from the man, who merely regarded him as an ordinary boy not worth his notice.

Deduction.—When he got near home, some five or six miles

OBSERVING THE MURDERER'S BOOTS

away, he came to a crowd round a cottage, where they had found the old woman (Margaret Crozier) who inhabited it lying murdered. All sorts of guesses were being hazarded as to who had done the deed, and suspicion seemed to centre on a small gang of three or four gipsies who were going about the country robbing and threatening death to anyone who made any report of their misdeeds.

The boy heard all these things, but presently he saw some peculiar footprints in the little garden of the cottage; the nail-marks agreed with those he had seen in the boots of the man on the moor, and he naturally deduced from these that the man might have something to do with the murder.

Chivalry.—The fact that it was a helpless old woman who had been murdered made the boy's chivalrous feeling rise against the murderer, whoever he might be.

Pluck and Self-Discipline, Alacrity.—So, although he knew that the friends of the murderer might kill him for giving information, he cast his fears on one side and went at once and told the constable of the footmarks in the garden, and where he could find the man who had made them—if he went immediately.

Health and Strength.—The man up on the moor had got so far from the scene of the murder, unseen (except by this one small boy), that he thought himself safe, and never thought of the boy being able to walk all the way to the scene of the murder and then to come back, as he did, with the police. So he took no precautions.

But the boy was a strong, healthy hill-boy, and did the journey rapidly and well, so that they found the man and captured him without difficulty.

The man was Willie Winter, a gipsy.

He was tried, found guilty, and hanged at Newcastle. His body was then brought and hung in a gibbet near the scene of the murder, as was the custom in those days, and the gibbet still stands to this day. Two of the gipsies who were his accomplices were caught with some of the stolen property, and were also executed at Newcastle.

Kind-heartedness.—But when the boy saw the murderer's body hanging there on the gibbet he was overcome with misery at having caused the death of a fellow-creature.

Saving Life.—However, the magistrate sent for him and complimented him on the great good he had done to his fellow-countrymen—probably saving some of their lives—by ridding the world of such a dangerous criminal.

Duty.—He said: "You have done your duty, although it caused you personally some danger and much distress. Still, you must not mind that—it was your duty to the King to help the police in getting justice done, and duty must always be carried out regardless of how much it costs you, even if you have to give up your life."

Example.—Thus the boy did every part of the duty of a Boy Scout without ever having been taught.

He exercised—Woodcraft; Observation, without being noticed; Deduction; Chivalry; Sense of duty; Endurance; Kind-heartedness.

He little thought that the act which he did entirely of his own accord would years afterwards be held up as an example to you other boys in teaching you to do your duty. In the same way you should remember your acts may be watched by others after you, and taken as an example, too. So try to do your duty the right way on all occasions.

CAMP FIRE YARN. No. 3

TESTS

Tenderfoot Test

BEFORE he becomes a Scout a boy must pass the Tenderfoot Test. This is a simple test just to show that he is worth his salt and means to stick to it. It is nothing very difficult and you will find all you want to know in this book.

You must be between 11 and 18 years of age.

Know the Scout Law and Promise, and understand their meanings. (See pages 17–19).

Know the salutes and their importance. (See page 20).

The woodcraft signs. (See page 31).

Clean a wound, and make and apply a dressing.

Know the composition and history of, and how to hoist, break and fly, the Union Jack. (See page 13).

Tie the following knots: reef, sheet bend, clove hitch, bowline, round turn and two half hitches, sheepshank, and understand their uses. (See pages 57–8).

Know how to whip the end of a rope. (See page 58).

When you have satisfied your Scoutmaster that you can do all these things and do them properly, you will be invested as a Scout and be entitled to wear the Scout badge in the button-hole of your coat, and on the left breast of your shirt when in uniform.

Scout Law

Scouts, all the world over, have unwritten laws which bind them just as much as if they had been printed in black and white.

They come down to us from old times.

The following are the rules which apply to Boy Scouts, and which you promise to obey when you are enrolled as a Scout, so it is as well that you should know all about them.

The Scout Law

1. **A Scout's Honour is to be Trusted.**

   If a Scout says "On my honour it is so," that means that it *is* so, just as if he had made a most solemn promise.

   Similarly, if a Scouter says to a Scout, "I trust you on your honour to do this," the Scout is bound to carry out the order to the very best of his ability, and to let nothing interfere with his doing so.

If a Scout were to break his honour by telling a lie, or by not
carrying out an order exactly when trusted on his honour
to do so, he may be directed to hand over his Scout badge,
and never to wear it again. He may also be directed to
cease to be a Scout.

2. **A Scout is Loyal to the Queen, his Country, his Scouters, his
   parents, his employers, and to those under him.**

   He must stick to them through thick and thin against anyone
   who is their enemy or who even talks badly of them.

3. **A Scout's Duty is to be useful and to Help Others.**

   And he is to do his duty before anything else, even though
   he gives up his own pleasure, or comfort, or safety to do it.
   When in difficulty to know which of two things to do, he
   must ask himself, "Which is my duty?" that is, "Which is
   best for other people?"—and do that one. He must Be
   Prepared at any time to save life, or to help injured persons.
   And *he must try his best to do at least one good turn* to
   somebody every day.

4. **A Scout is a Friend to All, and a Brother to Every Other
   Scout, no matter to what Country, Class or Creed the Other
   may belong.**

   Thus if a Scout meets another Scout, even though a stranger
   to him, he must speak to him, and help him in any way
   that he can, either to carry out the duty he is then doing,
   or by giving him food, or, as far as possible, anything that
   he may be in want of. A Scout must never be a SNOB.
   A snob is one who looks down upon another because he is
   poorer, or who is poor and resents another because he is
   rich. A Scout accepts the other man as he finds him, and
   makes the best of him.

   "Kim" was called by the Indians "Little friend of all the
   world," and that is the name that every Scout should earn
   for himself.

5. **A Scout is Courteous:** That is, he is polite to all—but
   especially to women and children, and old people and
   invalids, cripples, etc. And he must not take any reward
   for being helpful or courteous.

6. **A Scout is a Friend to Animals.** He should save them as
   far as possible from pain, and should not kill any animal
   unnecessarily, for it is one of God's creatures. Killing an
   animal for food or an animal which is harmful is allowable.

7. **A Scout Obeys Orders of his parents, Patrol Leader or Scout-master without question.**

Even if he gets an order he does not like he must do as sol-diers and sailors do, and as he would do for his Captain in a football team. He must carry it out all the same *because it is his duty*; and after he has done it he can come and state any reasons against it: but he must carry out the order at once. That is discipline.

8. **A Scout Smiles and Whistles under all difficulties.** When he gets an order he should obey it cheerily and readily, not in a slow, hang-dog sort of way.

Scouts never grouse at hardships, nor whine at each other nor grumble when put out, but go on whistling and smiling.

Scouts never use bad language.

The punishment for swearing or using bad language is for each offence a mug of cold water to be poured down the offender's sleeve by the other Scouts. It was the punishment invented by the old British scout, Captain John Smith, three hundred years ago.

9. **A Scout is Thrifty,** that is, he saves every penny he can, and puts it into the bank, so that he may have money to keep himself when out of work, and thus not make himself a burden to others; or that he may have money to give away to others when they need it.

10. **A Scout is Clean in Thought, Word and Deed,** that is, he looks down upon a silly youth who talks dirt, and he does not let himself give way to temptation either to talk it or to think, or to do anything dirty.

A Scout is clean-minded and manly.

Scout Promise

At the Investiture you will have to make the Scout Promise in front of the rest of the Troop.

The Scout Promise is:

"On my honour I promise that I will do my best—

To do my duty to God, and the Queen,
To help other people at all times,
To obey the Scout Law."

This is a very difficult Promise to keep, but it is a most serious one and no boy is a Scout unless he does his best to keep his Promise. All promises are important things and should never be broken, but when you promise on your honour to do a thing you would rather die than break such a promise. So you see Scouting is not only fun provided for you, but it also requires a lot from you and I know I can trust you to do everything you possibly can to keep your Scout Promise.

Scout's Salute and Sign

The three fingers held up (like the three points of a Scout's badge) is the Scout Salute and reminds a Scout of his three promises:

1. To do his duty to God, and the Queen.
2. To help other people at all times.
3. To obey the Scout Law.

All wearers of the Scout badge salute each other once a day. The first to salute should be the first to see the other Scout, irrespective of rank. Scouts will always salute as a token of respect, at the hoisting of the Union Flag; at the playing of the National Anthem; to the uncased National Colours; to Scout Flags, when carried ceremonially; and to all funerals.

On these occasions, if the Scouts are acting under orders, they obey the orders of the Scouter in charge as regards saluting or standing to the alert. If a Scout is not acting under orders he should salute independently. In all cases, Scouters if covered should salute.

The hand salute is only used when a Scout is not carrying his staff, and is always made with the right hand.

When carrying a staff the salute shown on page 141 is used for all occasions, and the Scout Sign is made with the left hand. When in uniform a Scout salutes whether he is wearing a hat or not, with one exception, namely, at religious services, when all Scouts must stand at the alert, instead of saluting.

Saluting when carrying a staff is done by bringing the left arm smartly across the body in a horizontal position, the fingers showing the Scout sign just touching the staff.

If a stranger makes the Scout's sign to you, you should acknowledge it at once by making the sign back to him, and then shake hands with the LEFT HAND. If he then shows his Scout's badge, or proves that he is a Scout, you must treat him as a brother-Scout, and help him in any way you can.

Investiture of Scouts

The Troop is formed in a horseshoe formation, with Scoutmaster and Assistant Scoutmaster in the gap.

The recruit with his Patrol Leader stands just inside the circle opposite to the Scoutmaster. The Assistant Scoutmaster holds the staff and hat of the recruit. When ordered to come forward by the Scoutmaster, the Patrol Leader brings the recruit to the centre. The Scoutmaster then asks: "Do you know what your honour is?"

The recruit replies: "Yes. It means that I can be trusted to be truthful and honest." (Or words to that effect.)

"Do you know the Scout Law?"—"Yes."

"Can I trust you, on your honour, to do your best—

To do your duty to God, and the Queen?
To help other people at all times?
To obey the Scout Law?"

The Recruit then makes the Scout sign, and so do the whole Troop whilst he says:

"On my honour I promise that I will do my best—

To do my duty to God, and the Queen,
To help other people at all times,
To obey the Scout Law."

Scoutmaster: "I trust you, on your honour, to keep this Promise. You are now one of the world-wide brotherhood of Scouts."

(If the boy has been a Cub, the wording should be, "You are now a Scout in the world-wide brotherhood.")

The Assistant Scoutmaster then puts on his hat and gives him his staff.

The Scoutmaster shakes hands with him with the left hand.

The new Scout faces about and salutes the Troop.

The Troop salute.

The Scoutmaster gives the word, "To your Patrol, quick march."

The Troop shoulder staffs, and the new Scout and his Patrol Leader march back to their Patrol.

When taking this Promise the Scout will stand holding his right hand raised level with his shoulder, palm to the front, thumb resting on the nail of the little finger, and the other three fingers upright, pointing upwards. The rest of the Troop do this with their disengaged hands.

This is called "The Scout Sign" and is given at the making of the Promise, and as a friendly greeting when not in uniform. When raised to the forehead, it is the "Salute."

CAMP FIRE YARN. No. 4

PATROL SYSTEM

THE Scout uniform is very like what my men used to wear when I commanded the South African Constabulary; they knew what was comfortable, serviceable and a good protection against the weather; so Scouts have much the same uniform.

Starting at the top, the broad-brimmed khaki hat is a good protection from the sun and rain. It is also useful to hide behind if you lie down and prop it up in front of you. It is kept on by a bootlace tied in a bow in front of the brim and going round the back of the head. This lace will come in handy in many ways when campaigning and you quickly want a strong tier. The hat has four dents in it, at the front, back and sides.

Then the scarf which is folded into a triangle with the point at the back of the neck. Every Group has its own scarf colour, and as the honour of your Group is bound up in the scarf, you must be very careful to keep it clean and tidy. It may be fastened at the throat by a knot or a woggle, which is some form of ring made of cord, metal or bone, or anything you like. The scarf is very useful for an emergency bandage or making a ladder, etc.

There are four different coloured shirts or jerseys allowed— khaki, grey, blue, or green, and each Group chooses which it will have. They are fine free-and-easy things and nothing could be more comfortable when the sleeves are rolled up, and all Scouts have them rolled up, unless it is very cold or their arms become too sunburnt, as a sign that they are ready to carry out their motto, "Be Prepared."

Shorts may be blue, khaki or grey (Scottish Scouts may wear the kilt and sporran). They give freedom to the legs and ventilation. Another advantage is that when the ground is wet, you can go about without stockings and none of your clothes gets damp. Damp clothes are dangerous and would soon make you ill.

Any plain stockings may be worn and they are kept up by garters with green tabs showing below the turn-over of the stocking top.

Badges

When you have been invested as a Scout you can go on to the next grade, that of Second Class Scout. For this you will learn the beginnings of many useful subjects. No Scout will want to remain

Second Class for longer than he need and so you will become a
First Class Scout as soon as you can. This will mean hard work
tackling Signalling, Map-reading, Hiking, Ambulance and many
other things. At the same time you can win proficiency badges
for your hobbies. Details of all these tests are to be found in *The
Scout's Book of Rules*. (Scout Shop, 1 6*d.*)

Scout's War Songs

1. *The Scout's chorus.* This is a chant that the Zulus used to
sing to their Chief.

> Leader (in a shrill kind of whine):
>   "Een gonyâma." "He is a Lion."
> Chorus (in astonishment):
>   "Gonyâma?" "A Lion."
> (with emphasis and rising energy and enthusiasm):
>   "Invooboo."   "No! He's greater than that;
>   he's a Hippopotamus."
>   "Ya bô."   "Yes, Sir!"
>   "Ya bô."   "Yes, Sir!"
>   "Invooboo!"   "He's a Hippopotamus!"

2. *The Scout's Rally.*
> To be shouted as a salute, or in a game, or at any time.
>   Leader: Be prepared!
>   Chorus: Zing-a-Zing!
>   Bom! Bom!
> (Stamp or bang something at the "Bom! Bom!")

The Patrol System

Each Troop is divided into Patrols of six to eight boys, and the
main object of the Patrol System is to give real responsibility to
as many boys as possible with a view to developing their charac-

ters. If the Scoutmaster gives his Patrol Leader real power, expects a great deal from him and leaves him a free hand in carrying out his work, he will have done more for that boy's character expansion than any amount of school training could ever do.

The Court of Honour is a most valuable aid to this end if fully made use of.

A Court of Honour is formed of the Scoutmaster and the Patrol Leaders, or, in the case of a small Troop, of the Patrol Leaders and Seconds. In many Courts the Scoutmaster attends the meetings, but does not vote. The Court of Honour decides rewards, punishments, programmes of work, camps and other questions affecting Troop management.

The members of the Court of Honour are pledged to secrecy; only those decisions which affect the whole Troop, e.g. appointments, competitions, etc., would be made public.

Patrol Leaders have in many cases formed themselves into a Court of Honour and carried on the Troop in the absence of the Scoutmaster.

A Word to Patrol Leaders

I want you Patrol Leaders to go on and train your Patrols in future entirely yourselves, because it is possible for you to get hold of each boy in your Patrol and make a good fellow of him. It is no use having one or two brilliant boys and the rest no good at all. You should try to make them all fairly good. The most important step to this is your own example, because what you do yourselves, your Scouts will do also. Show them that you can obey orders whether they are given by word of mouth or merely rules that are printed or written, and that you carry them out, whether your Scoutmaster is present or not. Show them that you can get badges for proficiency in different handicrafts, and your boys will, with very little persuasion, follow your lead.

But remember that you must give them the *lead* and not the *push*.

Patrol Signs

Each Troop is named after the place to which it belongs. Each Patrol in that Troop is named after an animal or bird. It is a good plan to choose only animals and birds found in the district. Thus the 33rd London Troop may have five Patrols which are respectively, the Curlews, the Bulldogs, the Owls, the Bats, the Cats.

Each Scout in a Patrol has his regular number, the Patrol Leader

SOME PATROL SIGNS AND CALLS

ALLIGATOR.
Harsh Bellow—"Hoo-ah-er."
GREEN AND KHAKI.

ANTELOPE.
High-pitched Roar—"Miaw ok."
NAVY AND WHITE.

BADGER.
Cry, like a stoat, in a high tone through the teeth—"Cheet-tt-tt."
PURPLE AND WHITE.

BAT.
Very High Squeak—"Pitz-pitz."
LIGHT BLUE AND BLACK.

BEAR.
Growl—"Boorrr."
BROWN AND BLACK.

BEAVER.
Slap made by clapping hands.
BLUE AND YELLOW.

BITTERN.
Cry—"Karr-Karr."
GREY AND GREEN.

BLACKBIRD.
Cry—"ForForForYee."
BLACK AND BROWN.

BUFFALO.
Lowing—"Um-maouw."
RED AND WHITE.

BULL.
Lowing—"Um-maouw."
RED.

BULLDOG.
Growl—"Graa-ow."
LIGHT BLUE AND BROWN.

CAPERCAILLIE.
Cry—"Petter Peller Peller."
BROWN AND GREY.

CAT.
Cry—"Meeaow."
GREY AND BROWN.

CHOUGH.
Cry—"Cree-a, Cree-a."
BLACK AND RED.

COBRA.
Hiss—"Pssst."
ORANGE AND BLACK.

COCKEREL.
Cry—"Cock-a-doodle doo."
RED AND BROWN.

CORMORANT.
Cry—"Cr-waar."
BLACK AND GREY.

CORNCRAKE.
Cry—"Crrrake."
PURPLE AND
GREY.

CUCKOO.
Call—"Cook-koo."
GREY.

CURLEW.
Whistle—"Curley."
GREEN.

DOVE.
Cry—"Coo-oo-oo."
GREY AND WHITE.

EAGLE.
Very Shrill Cry—
"Kreeee."
GREEN AND BLACK.

ELEPHANT.
Trumpeting Bellow—
"Trer-awmp-awmp-er."
PURPLE AND WHITE.

FALCON.
Cry—"Hik-hik-hik."
RED AND ORANGE.

FOX.
Bark—"Ha-ha."
YELLOW AND
GREEN.

GANNET.
Cry—"Aarrr."
YELLOW AND
NAVY.

GARGANEY.
Cry—"Heh." (nasal.)
BROWN AND GREEN.

GOLDEN PLOVER.
Cry—"Whistle up and
Down."
ORANGE AND GREY.

GROUSE.
Cry—"Go back,
Go back, Go back."
DARK AND LIGHT BROWN.

HAWK.
Cry—"Kreee."
PINK.

HERON.
Cry—"Quashk."
GREEN AND
GREY.

HIPPO.
Hiss—
"Brrussssh."
PINK AND BLACK.

HORSE.
Whinney—
"Hee-e-e-e."
BLACK AND WHITE.

HOUND.
Bark—
"Bawow-wow."
ORANGE.

HYENA.
Laughing—Cry—
"Ooowah-oowah-wah."
YELLOW AND WHITE.

JACKAL.
Laughing Cry—"Wah-
wah-wah-wah-wah-wah."
GREY AND BLACK.

KANGAROO.
Call—"Coo-ee."
RED AND GREY.

KESTREL.
Cry—"Kee-Kee"
ROYAL AND GREEN.

KINGFISHER.
Cry—"Chip Chip
Chip."
KINGFISHER BLUE.

LION.
Call—"Eu-ugh."
YELLOW AND RED.

MERLIN.
Cry—"Kik-Kik-
Kik."
ROYAL AND
MAROON.

MONGOOSE.
Squeak—"Cheep."
BROWN AND ORANGE.

NIGHTJAR.
Cry—"Churr-r-r-r"
(with tongue in roof
of mouth).
BLACK AND BROWN.

OTTER.
Cry—"Hoi-oi-oick."
BROWN AND WHITE.

OWL.
Whistle—
"Koot-koot-koo."
BLUE.

PANTHER.
*Tongue in side of
mouth—*"Keeook."
YELLOW.

PEACOCK.
Cry—"Bee-oik."
GREEN AND BLUE.

PEEWIT.
Whistle—"Tewitt."
GREEN AND WHITE.

PENGUIN.
Whistle—
"See-See."
WHITE AND
ORANGE.

PHEASANT.
Cry—"Cock Kerr."
BROWN AND YELLOW.

POCHARD.
Cry—"Err-Err."
CHESTNUT BROWN
AND GREY.

PUFFIN.
Cry—"Ugh, Ugh."
GREY AND YELLOW.

RAM.
Bleat—"Ba-a-a."
BROWN.

RATTLESNAKE.
Rattle a pebble in
a small -potted-
meat tin.
PINK AND WHITE.

RAVEN.
Cry—"Kar-kaw."
BLACK.

RHINO.
Roar—"War-war."
NAVY AND ORANGE.

SEA-GULL.
Mew—"Wee-wee-wee."
LIGHT BLUE AND
SCARLET.

SEAL.
Call—"Hark."
RED AND BLACK.

SKUA.
Cry—"Mee-Awk."
ROYAL AND
BROWN.

SNIPE.
Cry—"Tjick-Tjick."
ROYAL AND
SCARLET.

SPRINGBOK.
Cry—"Eugh Eugh."
SCARLET AND YELLOW

SQUIRREL.
Cry—"Nutt Nutt
Nutt."
GREY AND RED.

STAG.
Roar—"Baow."
VIOLET AND BLACK.

STARLING.
Cry—A drawn out
whistle up and
down the scale.
BLACK AND
YELLOW.

STONECHAT.
Cry—Clicking two
pebbles together.
CHESTNUT BROWN
AND BLACK.

STORK.
Cry—"Korrr."
BLUE AND WHITE.

STORMY PETREL.
Call—"Kekerekee."
NAVY AND GREY.

SWAN.
Cry—"S.S.S.S."
GREY AND SCARLET.

SWIFT.
Scream—"Quee."
NAVY.

TIGER.
Purr—"Grrao."
VIOLET.

WALRUS.
(Deep)—"Ouff."
WHITE AND
BROWN.

WIDGEON.
Cry—"Whee-ou."
BROWN.

WILD BOAR.
Grunt—"Broof-
broof."
GREY AND PINK.

WOLF.
Howl—"How-oooo."
YELLOW AND BLACK.

WOODCOCK.
Cry—A high-pitched
hissing whistle.
CHESTNUT BROWN
AND PURPLE.

WOODPECKER.
Laugh—*Chattering Yell.*—
"Heearfle-arfle-arfa."
GREEN AND PURPLE.

WOOD PIGEON.
Call—"Book-hooroo."
BLUE AND GREY.

being No. 1, the Second No. 2, and the Scouts have the consecutive numbers after these. Scouts usually work in pairs as comrades, Nos. 3 and 4 together, Nos. 5 and 6 together, and Nos. 7 and 8.

Each Patrol chooses its own motto, which generally applies in some way to the Patrol animal.

Each Scout in the Patrol has to be able to make the call of his Patrol animal—thus every Scout in the "Bulldogs" must be able to imitate the growl of the bulldog. This is the sign by which Scouts of a Patrol can communicate with each other when hiding or at night. No Scout is allowed to imitate the call of any Patrol except his own. The Patrol Leader calls up the Patrol at any time by sounding his whistle and uttering the call of the Patrol.

Also, when a Scout makes signs on the ground for others to read he also draws the head of the Patrol animal. Thus, if he wants to show that a certain road should not be followed he draws a sign across it, "Not to be followed," and adds the head of his Patrol animal to show which Patrol discovered that the road was no good, and his own number to the left of the head to show which Scout discovered it, thus:

Each Patrol Leader has a small white flag on his staff with the head of his patrol animal shown on it on both sides.

All these signs Scouts must be able to draw according to the Patrol to which they belong.

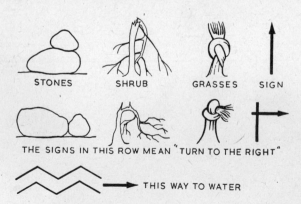

STONES   SHRUB   GRASSES   SIGN

THE SIGNS IN THIS ROW MEAN "TURN TO THE RIGHT"

THIS WAY TO WATER

Here are some Scout signs on the wall or ground, etc., close to the right-hand side of the road. These should never be made where they will damage or disfigure private property.

⟶   Road to be followed.

3⟶   Letter hidden three paces from here in the direction of the arrow.

⤬   This path not to be followed.

⊙   "I have gone home."

              (Signed) Patrol Leader of the Ravens 15th London Troop.

At night sticks with a wisp of grass round them or stones should be laid on the road in similar forms so that they can be felt with the hand.

CAMP FIRE YARN. No. 5

LIFE IN THE OPEN

THE native boys of the Zulu and Swazi tribes in South Africa learned to be scouts before they were allowed to be considered men, and they did it in this way. When a boy was about fifteen or sixteen he was taken by the men of his village, stripped of all clothes, and painted white from head to foot, and he was given a shield and one assegai or small spear, and he was turned out of the village and told that he would be killed if anyone caught him while he was still painted white. So the boy had to go off into the jungle and mountains and hide himself from other men until the white paint wore off, and this generally took about a month; so that all that time he had to look after himself and stalk game with his one assegai, and kill it and cut it up; he had to light his fire by means of rubbing sticks together in order to cook his meat; he had to make the skin of the animal into a covering for himself; and he had to know what kind of wild root, berries, and leaves are good for food as vegetables. If he was not able to do these things he died of starvation, or was killed by wild animals. If he succeeded in keeping himself alive, and was able to find his way back to his village, he returned when the white paint had worn off, and was then received with great rejoicings by his friends and relations, and was allowed to become a soldier of the tribe, since he had shown that he was able to look after himself.

And in South America the boys of the Yaghan tribe—down in the cold, rainy regions of Patagonia—wore no clothes, and before they were allowed to consider themselves men they had to undergo a test of pluck, which consisted in the boy driving a spear deep into his thigh and smiling all the time in spite of the pain.

It was a cruel test, but it shows that these savages understood how necessary it is that boys should be trained to manliness and not be allowed to drift into being poor-spirited wasters who can only look on at men's work.

The ancient British boys used to have the same kind of training before they were allowed to be considered men, and the training which we are now doing as Scouts is intended to fill that want as far as possible. If every boy works hard at this course and really learns all that we try to teach him, he will, at the end of it, have

32

some claim to call himself a scout and a man, and will find if ever he goes abroad, that he will have no difficulty in looking after himself.

I knew an old Boer who, after the South African War, said that he could not live in the country with the British, because when they arrived in the country they were so "stom," as he called it—i.e., so utterly stupid when living on the veldt that they did not know how to look after themselves, to make themselves comfortable in camp, to kill their food or to cook it, and they were always losing their way in the bush; he allowed that after six months or so the English soldiers got to learn how to manage for themselves fairly well if they lived so long, but that they often died, and they generally died through blundering about at the business end of the mule.

The truth is that, being brought up in a civilized country, men have no training whatever in looking after themselves out on the veldt, or in the backwoods, and the consequence is that when they go abroad they are for a long time perfectly helpless, and go through a lot of hardship and trouble which would not occur had they learned, while boys, how to look after themselves both in camp and when on patrol. They are just a lot of "tenderfoots."

They have never had to light a fire or to cook their own food : that has always been done for them. At home if they wanted water they merely had to turn on the tap, and had no idea of how to set about finding water in a desert place by looking at the grass, or bush, or by scratching at the sand till they began to find signs of dampness; and if they lost their way, or did not know the time, they merely had to "ask a policeman." They had always found houses to shelter them, and beds to lie in. They had never to manufacture these for themselves, nor to make their own boots or clothing. That is why a "tenderfoot" talks of "roughing it in camp"; but living in camp for a scout who knows the game, is by no means "roughing it." He knows how to make himself comfortable in a thousand small ways, and then, when he does come back to civilization, he enjoys it all the more for having seen a contrast; and even there he can do very much more for himself than the ordinary mortal, who has never really learned to provide for his own wants. The man who has had to turn his hand to many things as the scout does in camp finds that when he comes into civilization he is more easily able to obtain employment, because he is ready to turn his hand to whatever kind of work may turn up.

Exploration

A good form of scout work can be got by Scouts going about either as Patrols on an exploring expedition or in pairs like knight-errants of old on a pilgrimage through the country to find people wanting help and to help them. This can equally well be done with bicycles, or in the winter by skating along the canals.

Scouts in carrying out such a tramp should never, if possible, sleep under a roof—that is to say, on fine nights they would sleep in the open wherever they may be; or, in bad weather, would get leave to occupy a hay loft or barn.

You should on all occasions take a map with you, and find your way by it, as far as possible, without having to ask the way of passers-by. You would, of course, have to do your daily good turn whenever opportunity presented itself, but besides that, you should do good turns to farmers and others who may allow you the use of their barns, and so on, as a return for their kindness.

As a rule you should have some object in your expedition; that is to say, if you are a Patrol of town boys, you would go off with the idea of scouting some special spot, say a mountain, or a famous lake, or possibly some old castle or battlefield, or a seaside beach. Or you may be on your way to join one of the larger camps.

If, on the other hand, you are a Patrol from the country, you can make your way up to a big town, with the idea of going to see its buildings, and its Zoological Gardens, circuses, museums, etc. And you should notice everything as you go along the roads, and remember, as far as possible, all your journey, so that you could give directions to anybody else who wanted to follow that road afterwards. And make a map. Explorers, of course, keep a log or journal, giving a short account of each day's journey, with sketches or photos of any interesting things they see.

Mountaineering

A good deal of interesting mountaineering can be done in the British Isles and many places abroad if you know about where to go, and it is grand sport, and brings out into practice all your scoutcraft to enable you to find your way, and to make yourself comfortable in camp.

You are, of course, continually losing your direction, because, moving up and down in the deep gullies of the mountain-side, you lose sight of the landmarks which usually guide you, so that you have to watch your direction by the sun and by your compass, and keep on estimating in what direction your proper line of travel lies.

Then, again, you are very liable to be caught in fogs and mists, which are at all times upsetting to the calculations even of men who know every inch of the country. I had such an experience in Scotland one year, when, in company with a Highlander who knew the ground, I got lost in the mist. But, supposing that he knew the way, I committed myself entirely to his guidance, and after going some distance I felt bound to remark to him that I noticed the wind had suddenly changed, for it had been blowing from our left when we started, and was now blowing hard on our right cheek. However, he seemed in no way nonplussed, and led on. Presently, I remarked that the wind was blowing behind us, so that either the wind, or the mountain, or we ourselves were turning round. And eventually it proved as I suggested, that it was not the wind that had turned, or the mountain; it was ourselves who had wandered round in a complete circle, and were almost back at the point we started from within an hour.

The Scouts working on a mountain ought to practise the art of roping themselves together, as mountaineers do on icy slopes to save themselves from falling into holes in the snow and slipping down precipices. When roped together in this way, supposing that one man falls, the weight of the others will save him from going down into the depths.

When roped together each man has about 14 feet between himself and the next man. The rope is fastened round his waist by a loop or bowline, the knot being on his left side. Each man has to keep back off the man in front of him, so that the rope is tight all the time; then, if one falls or slips the others lean away from him with all their weight, and hold him up till he regains his footing. A loop takes up about 4 ft. 6 in. of rope, and should be a "bowline" at the ends of the rope, and a "middleman's knot" or "man harness hitch" for central men on the rope.

Patrolling

Scouts generally go about scouting in pairs, or sometimes singly; if more go together they are called a Patrol. When they are patrolling the Scouts of a Patrol hardly ever move close together; they are spread out so as to see more country, and so that if cut off or ambuscaded by an enemy, they will not all get caught, but some will get away to give information. A Patrol of six Scouts working in open country would usually move in this sort of formation, in the shape of a kite with the Patrol Leader in the centre; if going along a street or road the Patrol would move in a similar

way, the flank Scouts keeping close to the hedges or walls. No. 2
Scout is in front, Nos. 5 and 4 to the right and left, No. 3 to the
rear, and No. 6 with the Leader (No. 1) in the centre.

PATROL IN THE OPEN

If there are, say, eight in the Patrol, the Patrol Leader should
take the tenderfoot, No. 2 should take No. 6 and No. 3 should
take No. 7 along with them.

Patrols when going across open country where they are likely
to be seen by enemies or animals should get over it as quickly as
possible, i.e. by moving at the Scout pace, walking and running
alternately from one point of cover to another. As soon as they
are hidden in cover they can rest and look round before making
the next move. If as leading Scout you get out of sight of your
Patrol, you should, in passing thick bushes, reeds, etc., bend
branches or stems of reeds and grass every few yards making the
heads point *forward* to show your path, for in this way you can
always find your way back again, or the Patrol or anyone coming

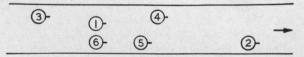

PATROL ON A ROAD OR STREET

after you can easily follow up, and they can judge from the freshness of the grass pretty well how long ago it was you passed that
way. Or you can make marks in the sand, or lay stones, or show
which way you have gone by the signs which I have given you.

When a Troop is marching as a body along a road it is well to "divide the road." That is for the Scouts to move in a single file along each side of the road. In this way they don't suffer from dust; and they don't interfere with the traffic.

Night Work

Scouts must be able to find their way equally well by night as by day. But unless they practise it frequently, fellows are very apt to lose themselves by night, distances seem greater, and landmarks are hard to see. Also you are apt to make more noise than by day, in walking along, by accidentally treading on dry sticks, kicking stones, etc.

If you are watching for an enemy at night, you have to trust much more to your ears than to your eyes, and also to your nose, for a Scout who is well-practised at smelling out things, and who has not damaged his sense of smell by smoking, can often smell an enemy a good distance away. I have done it many times myself, and found it of the greatest value.

When patrolling at night, Scouts keep closer together than by day, and in very dark places, such as woods, etc., they should keep touch with each other by each catching hold of the end of the next Scout's staff.

When working singly the Scout's staff is most useful for feeling the way in the dark, and pushing aside dry branches, etc.

Scouts working apart from each other in the dark keep up communication by occasionally giving the call of their Patrol animal. An enemy would thus not be made suspicious.

All Scouts have to guide themselves very much by the stars at night, and should normally work in Patrols or in pairs.

Finding the Way

Among the Red Indian scouts the man who was good at finding his way in a strange country was termed a "Pathfinder," which was with them a name of great honour, because a scout who cannot find his way is of very little use.

Many a "tenderfoot" has got lost in the veldt or forest, and has never been seen again, through not having learned a little scouting, or what is called "eye for a country" when a boy. I have known many instances of it myself.

In one case a man got off a coach, which was driving through the bush in Matabeleland, for a few minutes, while the mules were being changed. He apparently walked off a few yards into the bush, and when the coach was ready to start they called for him in every direction, and searched for him, but were unable to find him; and at last, the coach, being unable to wait any longer, pursued its journey, leaving word for the lost man to be sought for. Full search was made for him; his tracks were followed as fas as they could be, in the very difficult soil of that country, but he was not found for weeks afterwards, and then his dead body was discovered nearly fifteen miles away from where he started, and close to the road.

It often happens that when you are tramping along alone through the bush, or even in a town, you become careless in noticing what direction you are moving in; that is, you frequently change it to get round a fallen tree, or some rocks, or some other obstacle, and having passed it, you do not take up exactly the correct direction again; a man's inclination somehow is to keep edging to his right, and the consequence is that when you think you are going straight, you are really not doing so at all; unless you watch the sun, or your compass, or your landmarks, you are very apt to find yourself going round in a big circle after a short time.

In such a case a "tenderfoot," when he suddenly finds himself out of his bearings, and lost alone in the desert or forest, at once loses his head and gets excited, and probably begins to run, when the right thing to do is to force yourself to keep cool and give yourself something useful to do—that is, to track your own spoor back again; or, if you fail, start getting firewood for making signal fires to direct those who are looking for you.

The main point is not to get lost in the first instance.

Every old scout on first turning out in the morning notices which way the wind is blowing.

When you start out for a walk or on patrol, you should notice which direction, by the compass, you start in, and also notice which direction the wind is blowing, as that would be a great help to you in keeping your direction, especially if you have not got a compass, or if the sun is not shining.

Then you should notice all landmarks for finding your way, that is, in the country notice any hills or prominent towers, steeples, curious trees, rocks, gates, mounds, bridges and so on; any points, in fact, by which you could find your way back again, or by which you could instruct anyone to go the same line which you have gone. If you notice your landmarks going out you can always find your way back by them, but you should take care occasionally to look back at them after passing them, so that you get to know their appearance for your return journey. The same holds good when you are in a town, or when you arrive in a new town by train; the moment you step out from the station notice where the sun is, or which way the smoke is blowing. Also notice your landmarks, which would be prominent buildings, churches, factory chimneys, names of streets and shops, etc., so that when you have gone down numerous streets you can turn round and find your way back again to the station without any difficulty. It is wonderfully easy when you have practised it a little, yet many people get lost when they have turned a few corners in a town which they do not know.

The way to find which way the wind is blowing if there is only very light air is to throw up little bits of dry grass, or to hold up a handful of light dust and let it fall, or to suck your thumb and wet it all round and let the wind blow on it, and the cold side of it will then tell you which way the wind is blowing. When you are acting as scout to find the way for a party you should move ahead of them and fix your whole attention on what you are doing, because you have to go by the very smallest signs, and if you get talking and thinking of other things you are very apt to miss them.

Finding the North

Every sailor boy knows the points of the compass by heart, and so should a Scout. I have talked a good deal about the north, and you will understand that it is a most important help to a Scout in pathfinding to know the direction of the north.

If you have not a compass the sun will tell you by day where the north is, and the moon and the stars by night.

At six o'clock in the morning (Greenwich time) the sun is east, at nine he is south-east, at noon he is south, at three o'clock in the afternoon he is south-west, and at six o'clock he is west. In winter he will have set long before six o'clock, but he will not have reached west when he is set. These facts apply to England and only roughly. You must allow for Summer Time.

The Phœnicians who sailed Africa in ancient times noticed that when they started the sun rose on their left-hand side—they were going south. Then they reported that they got to a strange country where the sun got up in the wrong quarter, namely, on their right hand. The truth was that they had gone round the Cape of Good Hope and were steering north again up the east side of Africa.

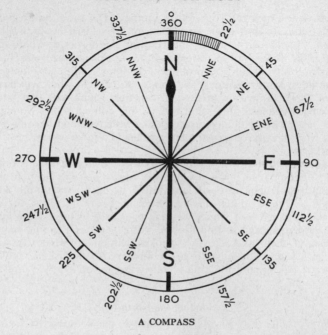

A COMPASS

To find the south at any time of day by the sun—hold your watch flat, face upwards, so that the sun shines on it. Turn it round till the hour hand points at the sun. Then without moving the

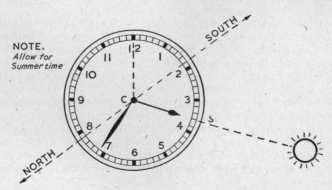

watch, lay the edge of a piece of paper or a pencil across the face of the watch so that it rests on the centre of the dial and points out half-way between the Figure XII and the hour hand. The line given by that pencil will be the true south and north line. This applies only in the Northern Hemisphere. In the Southern turn the XII, instead of the hand, to the sun, and the south and north line will then lie between the two as before. Again, allow for Summer Time.

THE STARS appear to circle over us during the night, which is really due to our earth turning round under them.

There are various groups which have got names given to them

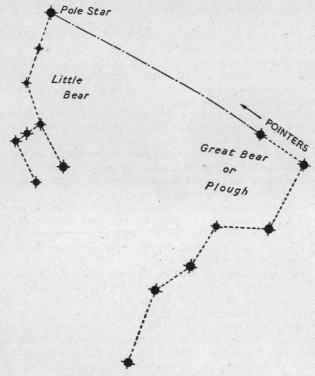

THE PLOUGH (OR "GREAT BEAR"),
THE POLE STAR AND THE "LITTLE BEAR."

because they seem to make some kind of pictures or "sky-signs" of men and animals.

The "Plough" is an easy one to find, being shaped something like a plough. And it is the most useful one for a Scout to know, because in the northern part of the world it shows him exactly where the north is. The Plough is also called the "Great Bear," and the four stars in the curve make its tail. It is the only bear I know that wears a long tail.

The two stars in the Plough called the "Pointers" point out where the North or Pole Star is. All the stars and constellations appear to move round, as I have said, during the night, but the Pole Star remains fixed in the north. There is also the "Little Bear" near the Great Bear, and the last star in his tail is the North or Pole Star.

The sky may be compared to an umbrella over you. The pole star is where the stick goes through the centre of it.

A real umbrella has been made with all the stars marked on it in their proper places. If you stand under it and twist it slowly round you see exactly how the stars quietly go round, but the pole star remains steady in the middle.

Then another set of stars or "constellation," as it is called, represents a man wearing a sword and belt, and is named "Orion." It is easily recognised by the three stars in line, which are the belt, and three smaller stars in another line, close by, which are the sword. Then two stars to right and left below the sword are his feet, while two more above the belt are his shoulders, and a group of three small stars between them make his head.

Now the great point about Orion is that by him you can always tell which way the north or pole star lies, and you can see him whether you are in the south or the north part of the world. The Great Bear you only see when you are in the north, and the Southern Cross when you are in the south.

If you draw a line, by holding up your staff against the sky, from the centre star of Orion's belt through the centre of his head, and carry that line on through two big stars till it comes to a third, that third one is the north or pole star.

Roughly, Orion's sword—the three small stars—points north.

The Zulus' scouts call Orion's belt and sword the "Ingolubu," or three pigs pursued by three dogs. The Masai in East Africa say that the three stars in Orion's belt are three bachelors being followed by three old maids. You see, scouts all know Orion, though under different names.

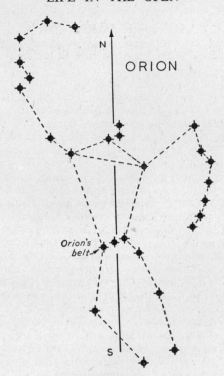

ORION

N

S

Orion's belt

**ORION AND HIS SWORD ALWAYS POINT
TO THE NORTH AND SOUTH POLES**

On the south side of the world, that is in South Africa, South America, New Zealand and Australia, the Plough or Great Bear is not visible, but the Southern Cross is seen. The Southern Cross is a good guide as to where the exact south is, which, of course, tells a scout just as much as the Great Bear in the north pointing to the North Star.

CAMP FIRE YARN. No. 6

SEA SCOUTS AND AIR SCOUTS

Old Sea-dogs

IN the days of Queen Elizabeth the First, some four hundred years ago, the sailors of Spain, of Britain, of Holland, and of Portugal were all making themselves famous for their daring voyages in small sailing ships across unknown oceans, by which they kept discovering new lands for their country in distant corners of the world.

There was one small cabin-boy on a coasting brig in the English Channel who used to long to become one of these discoverers, but when he looked at the practical side of the question, it seemed hopeless for a poor little chap like him ever to hope to rise in the world beyond his present hard life in the wretched little coaster, living on bad food and getting, as a rule, more kicks than halfpence.

But it shows you how the poorest boy can get on if he only puts his back into it. Young Drake—for that was his name—did get on, in spite of his difficulties: he worked hard at his duty, till his officers saw that he meant to get on and they promoted him, and in the end he became a captain of two small ships, one of seventy, the other of thirty tons; and with these he sailed to fight the Spaniards, who were at that time our enemies, away across the ocean in Central America. He not only fought them, but was successful in taking some of their ships and a great deal of valuable booty from their towns. On his return home he was promoted to command a larger expedition of five ships, the biggest of which, however, was only one hundred tons, and the smallest was fifteen tons. These were considered fine ships in those days, but were no bigger than our coasting schooners and fishing smacks of to-day.

With these he sailed down the West Coast of Africa, then across to Brazil and down the South American Coast till he rounded the end of it through the dangerous and difficult Straits of Magellan into the Pacific. He coasted up the western side of America as far as California, and then struck across the ocean to India, and thence via the Cape of Good Hope to England. This voyage took him nearly three years to complete. His good ship, the *Golden Hind,* though much battered and wounded with war and weather, was received with much honour at Deptford. The Queen herself went on board, and while there she showed such pleasure at

Drake's good work that she knighted him, using his own well-worn sword to make him Sir Francis Drake.

Nelson

Two hundred years after Drake came Nelson. He was the son of a clergyman in Norfolk—a poor sickly little fellow, and was for a time in the Merchant Service. His first step to greatness was when the ship which he was in captured an enemy's ship, and the first lieutenant was ordered to take a boat and some men and go aboard the prize.

But owing to the heavy sea which was running the officer gave up the attempt as too dangerous, whereupon Nelson, like a good scout, stepped forward and offered to go. He succeeded, and was thence marked as a good officer.

Every boy knows how, after a splendid career of fighting for England, he at last won the great sea-battle of Trafalgar against the French and Spanish fleets, and fell mortally wounded in the hour of victory.

But his work and that of other great sea captains who served with him completed the supremacy of the British navy at sea begun by Drake and the sea-dogs of his time. The navies of our enemies were entirely swept from off the seas, and their merchant ships could only carry on their trade so long as their countries remained at peace with Great Britain.

And that supremacy has meant the Freedom of the Seas to all peaceful traders.

The sailor has a grand life of it, continually visiting strange and interesting lands, with a good ship to manœuvre through distant oceans, with plenty of contests with tides and winds. A free, open, and healthy life which breeds cheery handiness and pluck, such as make a sailor so deservedly loved by all—and all the time he is doing grand work for his country.

Watermanship

It is very necessary for a Scout to be able to swim, for he never knows when he may have to cross a river, to swim for his life, or to plunge in to save someone from drowning. So those of you who cannot swim should make it your business to begin at once and learn; it is not very difficult.

Also, a Scout should be able to manage a boat, to bring it properly alongside the ship or pier, that is, either by rowing it or

steering it in a wide circle so that it comes up alongside with its head pointing the same way as the bow of the ship or towards the current. You should be able to row one oar in time with the rest of the boat's crew, or to scull a pair of oars, or to scull a boat by screwing a single oar over the stern. In rowing, the object of feathering, or turning the blade of the oar flat when it is out of the water, is to save it from catching the wind and thereby checking the pace of the boat. You should know how to throw a coil of rope so as to fling it on to another boat or wharf, or how to catch and make fast a rope thrown to you. Also you should know how to make a raft out of any materials that you can get hold of, such as planks, logs, barrels, sacks of straw, and so on, for often you may want to cross a river with your food and baggage where no boats are available, or you may be in a shipwreck where nobody can make a raft for saving themselves. You should also know how to throw a lifebuoy or a life-line to a drowning man. These things can only be learned by practice.

As a Scout you must know how to fish, else you would find yourself very helpless, and perhaps starving, on a river which is full of food for you if you were only able to catch it.

The first scouting that I did as a boy was sea scouting, in a sailing boat in which, with my brothers, I cruised round the coasts of England and Scotland. I had the time of my life. I hope you will enjoy it as much as I did when you take it up.

Canoeing

It is possible for a boy who is intelligent and possesses a few tools to make his own canoe. The Scout Shop at 25, Buckingham Palace Road, London, S.W.1, can supply full instructions and drawings for building two really serviceable canoes of modern design. For touring the P.B.K. 13 is recommended, being a fast single-seater 13 ft. in length. If, however, a two-seater is required, the P.B.K. 20 is a stable 15-ft. craft that can be easily paddled, and is adaptable to sailing. Both are designed to give maximum safety on sea or inland waters and to carry normal camping kit.

Air Scouts

When the first Scout Camp was held at Brownsea Island, very few people really thought that the aeroplane would conquer the air. They had heard of some queer experiments carried out by Wilbur and Orville Wright with gliders and of their attempts with some kind of air-machine; but no one dreamt that within a lifetime the aeroplane would become a means of travel, and a new means for bringing death to thousands.

Of course there had been balloon flights for many years. Actually the first living creatures to go up in a balloon were a sheep, a cock and a duck, which were taken up by a balloon in 1783; they all survived! The first man to trust himself to a balloon was de Rozier, the month after the animals had shown the way.

The trouble with a balloon is that you can't control it very much, and man wanted some kind of air-machine which could be guided like a ship from place to place. It was not until the engine was used in air experiments that the way was at last opened for advance. One line of experiment led to the airship, and the first airship flight across the Atlantic and back to England was made in the *R. 34* in 1919.

The aeroplane was the other line of experiment. Here the Wright Brothers showed the way, but it was not until July 25th, 1909, when the Frenchman, Bleriot, crossed the Channel in 35 minutes from Calais to Dover, that people began to take serious notice of the aeroplane.

From that time onwards, progress was rapid, and it is marked by a series of flights which have made history as much as Drake's voyage round the world in the *Golden Hind*.

Amongst these epoch-making flights may be mentioned the first non-stop crossing of the Atlantic by two British airmen, Sir John Alcock and Sir Arthur Whitten Brown in 1919, and in the same year the first flight from England to Australia by Sir Ross and Sir Keith Smith.

With good reason we are apt to think of the aeroplane as a weapon of destruction; but it has many valuable uses for civilisation. For instance, in Canada vast tracts of unexplored territory in the north have been photographed and mapped; mining machinery has been transported to out-of-the-way places; traders and settlers, who are cut off by great distances from supplies and friends, can receive food, letters and newspapers by 'plane. In Australia, doctors travel enormous distances by 'plane to help sick people, and flying ambulances can bring them into hospital. Fires in great forest areas can be spotted quickly by the airman and the best means devised for fighting the fires. Even fishermen can be helped because from a height it is possible for the airmen to see where the shoals of fish are to be found.

Insect pests which attack and ruin crops can be killed by "dusting" from the air; rice and grass seeds have been sown over vast areas in a short time.

All kinds of interesting discoveries have been made not only about unexplored parts of the earth, but about the past, for some things—markings of ancient dwellings and settlements, for instance—show up more clearly when seen and photographed from the air. So you see there is still plenty of pioneering and romance in the new element man has conquered!

Air Scouts are now part of our Scouting organisation. Just like Sea Scouts, they have to be as well-trained in ordinary Scouting on land as the rest of us; for all Scouts need to be observant and resourceful. So if you are attracted to the work and excitement of being an airman, you now have the chance, as a Scout, of making a beginning.

Further information about Sea Scouts, and Air Scouts, can be obtained from the Training Secretary, Boy Scouts Association, 25, Buckingham Palace Road, London, S.W.1.

SIGNALS AND COMMANDS

SCOUTS have to be very clever at passing news secretly from one place to another, or signalling to each other.

Before the siege of Mafeking commenced, I received a secret message from some unknown friend in the Transvaal, who sent me news of the Boers' plans against the place, and the numbers that they were getting together of men, horses and guns. This news came to me by means of a very small letter which was rolled up in a little ball, the size of a pill, and put inside a tiny hole in a rough walking-stick, and plugged in there with wax. The stick was given to a native, who merely had orders to come into Mafeking and give me the stick as a present. Naturally, when he brought me this stick, and said it was from another white man, I guessed there must be something inside it, and soon found this very important letter.

Also I received another letter from a friend, which was written in Hindustani language, but in English writing, so that anybody reading it would be quite puzzled as to what language it was written in; but to me it was all as clear as daylight.

Then, when we sent letters out from Mafeking, we used to give them to natives who were able to creep out between the Boer outposts, and, once through the line of sentries, the Boers mistook them for their own natives, and took no further notice of them. They carried their letters in this way. The letters were all written on thin paper in small envelopes, and half a dozen letters or more would be crumpled up tightly into a little ball, and then rolled up into a piece of lead paper, such as tea is packed in. The native scout would carry a number of these little balls in his hand, and hanging round his neck loosely by strings. Then, if he saw he was in danger of being captured by a Boer, he would drop all the balls on the ground, where they looked exactly like so many stones, and he would notice the landmarks from two or three points round about him, by which he would be able again to find the exact spot where the letters were lying; then he would walk boldly on until accosted by the Boer, who, if he searched him, would find nothing suspicious about him. He would then wait about for perhaps a day or two until the coast was clear, and come back to the spot where the landmarks told him the letters were lying.

"Landmarks," you may remember, mean any objects—like

trees, mounds, rocks or other details—which do not move away, and act as sign-posts for a scout, who notices and remembers them.

Signalling

Captain John Smith was one of the first to make use of signals to express regular words, three hundred years ago.

He was then fighting on the side of the Austrians against the Turks. He thought it wicked for Christian men to fight against Christians if it could possibly be avoided, but he would help any Christian, although a foreigner, to fight against a heathen; so he joined the Austrians against the Turks.

He invented a system of showing lights at night with torches which when held in certain positions with each other meant certain words.

Several officers in the Austrian forces practised these signals till they knew them.

On one occasion one of these officers was besieged by the Turks. John Smith brought a force to help him, and arrived on a hill near the town in the night. Here he made a number of torch signals, which were read by the officer inside, and they told him what to do. Then Smith attacked the enemy in the rear, and this enabled the garrison to break out successfully.

Signalling cannot be learned in a day, but it is well worth learning. It is of course good fun to be able to talk to your pal in this way across the street without other people understanding what you are talking about; but I have found it really valuable on more than one occasion for communicating with a friend out in the wild, once when we were on separate mountains and another time on opposite sides of a big river, and when one of us had urgent and important news to communicate.

Sound Signals

In the American Civil War, Captain Clowry, a scout officer, wanted to give warning to a large force of his own army that the enemy were going to attack it unexpectedly during the night; but he could not get to his friends because there was a flooded river between them which he could not cross, and a storm of rain was going on.

What would you have done if you had been he?

A good idea struck him. He got hold of an old railway engine that was standing near him. He lit the fire and got up steam in her, and then started to blow the whistle with short and long blasts—what is called the Morse alphabet. Soon his friends heard and understood, and answered back with a bugle. And he then spelt out a message of warning to them, which they read and acted upon. And so their force of 20,000 men was saved from surprise.

Every Scout ought to learn the "dot and dash," or Morse method of signalling, because it comes in most useful whenever you want to send messages some distance by flag signalling, as in the Army and Navy, and it is also useful in getting you employ-ment as a telegraphist. It is not difficult to learn if you set about it with a will. I found it most useful once during the Boer War. My column had been trying to get past a Boer force which was holding a pass in the mountains. Finding they were too strong for us, we gave it up late in the evening, and, leaving a lot of fires alight, as if we were in camp in front of them, we moved during the night by a rapid march right round the end of the mountain range, and by daylight next day we were exactly in rear of them without their knowing it. We then found a telegraph line, evi-dently leading from them to their headquarters some fifty miles farther off, so we sat down by the telegraph wire and attached our own little wire to it and read all the messages they were sending, and they gave us most valuable information. But we should not have been able to do that had it not been that some of our scouts could read the Morse code.

Then the semaphore signalling, which is done by waving your arms at different angles to each other, is most useful and quite easy to learn. Here you have all the different letters, and the different angles at which you have to put your arms to represent those letters; and, though it looks complicated in the picture, when you come to work it out you will find it is very simple. The signs are shown as they appear to a "reader."

For all letters from A to G one arm only is used, making an eighth of a circle for each letter in succession. Then from H to N (except J), the right arm stands at A, while the left moves round the circle again for the other letters. From O to S the right arm stands at B, and the left arm moves round as before. For T, U, Y, and the "erase," the right arm stands at C, the left moving to the next point of the circle successively.

The letters A to I also mean the figures 1 to 9 (K standing for 0)—if you make the numerical sign to show that you are going to send numbers, followed by the alphabetical sign (J) when the figures are finished. They will be checked by being repeated back by the *receiving* station. Should figures be wrongly repeated by

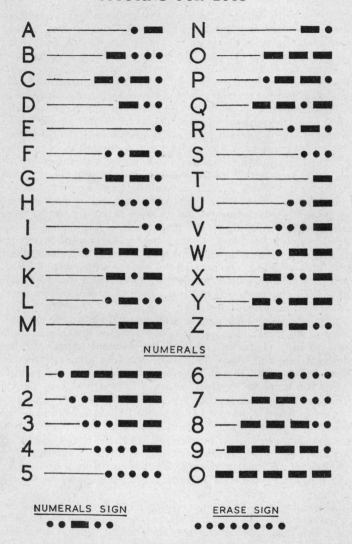

NUMERALS

NUMERALS SIGN

ERASE SIGN

THE MORSE CODE

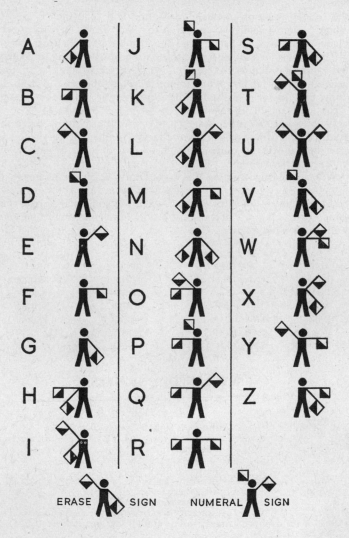

THE SEMAPHORE CODE

the *receiving* station, the *sending* station will send the "Erase or
Annul" sign (which is answered by A, which is called the
General Answer), and then send the group of figures again.

The sender must always face the station he is sending to. When
the *receiving* station has read a word correctly, they send the
general answer. If any word is not received, the *sending* station
know that the *receiving* station have not read it and so they go on
repeating it until it is answered.

If you want to write a despatch that will puzzle most people to
read, use the Morse or Semaphore letters in place of the ordinary
alphabet. It will be quite readable to any of your friends who
understand signalling.

When you are signalling it is great fun to learn the names that
signallers give to letters. These are used because it is easy to mistake one spoken letter for another when the sounds are much the
same, such as B and P. This is useful too, in telephoning when you
want to spell out a name.

A	ABLE	H	HOW	O	OBOE	V	VICTOR
B	BAKER	I	ITEM	P	PETER	W	WILLIAM
C	CHARLIE	J	JIG	Q	QUEEN	X	X-RAY
D	DOG	K	KING	R	ROGER	Y	YOKE
E	EASY	L	LOVE	S	SUGAR	Z	ZEBRA
F	FOX	M	MIKE	T	TARE		
G	GEORGE	N	NAN	U	UNCLE		

MISCELLANEOUS SIGNALS

SIGNAL.	MEANING AND USE.
VE, VE, VE.	Calling up signal.
K.	Carry on (answer to VE if ready to receive message).
Q.	Wait (answer to VE if not ready to receive message).
T (Morse). A (Sema-phore).	General answer (used to answer all signals un-less otherwise stated).
AR.	End of message signal.
R.	Message received correctly (answer to AR).
8 dots, or (Semaphore) opposite of L.	Erase (to erase anything sent incorrectly).
GB.	"Good-bye" (used when a station is going to close down).

Commands and Signals

Each Patrol Leader should provide himself with a whistle and a lanyard or cord for keeping it. The following commands and signals should be at your fingers'-ends, so that you can teach them to your Patrol, and know how to order it properly.

WORDS OF COMMAND

"Fall in" (in line).

"Alert" (stand up smartly).

"Easy" (stand at ease).

"Sit easy" (sit or lie down without leaving the ranks).

"Dismiss" (break off).

"Right turn" (or left turn); (each Scout turns accordingly).

"Patrol right turn" (or left turn); (each Patrol with its Scouts in line wheels to that hand).

"Quick march" (walk smartly, stepping off on the left foot).

"Double" (run at smart pace, arms hanging loose).

"Scout pace" (walk so many paces and jog so many paces alternately).

SIGNALS AND SIGNS

When a Scoutmaster wants to call his Troop together he whistles "The Scout's Call," or uses a special Troop call.

Patrol Leaders thereupon call together their Patrols by giving their Patrol cry. Then they double their Patrol to the Scoutmaster.

Here are some whistle signals:

1. One long blast means "Silence," "Alert," "Look out for my next signal."

2. A succession of long, slow blasts means "Go out," "Get farther away," or "Advance," "Extend," "Scatter."

3. A succession of short, sharp blasts means "Rally," "Close in," "Come together," "Fall in."

4. A succession of short and long blasts alternately means "Alarm," "Look out," "Be ready," "Man your alarm posts."

5. Three short blasts, followed by one long one from Scoutmaster calls up the Patrol Leaders—i.e. "Leaders come here!"

Any signal must be instantly obeyed at the double as fast as ever you can run—no matter what other job you may be doing at the time.

PIONEERING

Knot-tying

PIONEERS are men who go ahead to open up a way in the jungles or elsewhere for those coming after them.

When I was on service on the West Coast of Africa, I had command of a large force of native scouts, and, like all scouts, we tried to make ourselves useful in every way to our main army, which was coming along behind us. So not only did we look out for the enemy and watch his moves, but we also did what we could to improve the road for our own army, since it was merely a narrow track through thick jungle and swamps. That is, we became pioneers as well as scouts. In the course of our march we built nearly two hundred bridges of timber over streams. But

when I first set the scouts to do this most important work I found that, out of the thousand men, a great many did not know how to use an axe to cut down the trees, and, except one company of about sixty men, none knew how to make knots—even bad knots. So they were quite useless for building bridges, as this had to be done by tying poles together.

So every Scout ought to be able to tie knots.

To tie a knot seems to be a simple thing, and yet there are right ways and wrong ways of doing it, and Scouts ought to know the right way. Very often it may happen that lives depend on a knot being properly tied.

The right kind of knot to tie is one which you can be certain will hold under any amount of strain, and which you can always undo easily if you wish to.

A bad knot is one which slips away when a hard pull comes on it, or which gets jammed so tight that you cannot untie it.

The best way to learn is to get a fellow who knows to show you.

56

1. THE REEF KNOT, for tying two ropes together under strain, as in tying up a parcel. Being a flat knot, it is much used in ambulance work. The best simple knot, as it will not slip and is easy to untie.

2. SHEET BEND, or common bend, for joining ropes of equal or unequal thickness together. Make loop with one rope and pass other end through and round whole loop and bend it under its own standing part.

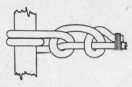

3. HALF HITCH, made by passing rope-end round standing part and behind itself. If free end is turned back and forms a loop, the hitch can be easily loosened. A round turn and two half hitches are used for tying a rope to a spar.

4. THE SHEEPSHANK, for shortening ropes. Gather up the amount to be shortened as in illustration. Then make a half hitch round each of the bends.

5. THE BOWLINE, a loop that will not slip, to tie round a person being lowered from a building, etc. Form a loop, then in the standing part form a second and smaller loop. Through this pass the end of the large loop and behind the standing part and down through the small loop.

s.b.—3

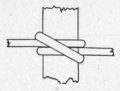

6. CLOVE HITCH, for fastening a rope to a spar. Either end will stand a strain without slipping, either lengthways or downwards.

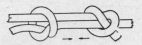

7. FISHERMAN'S KNOT is favoured by anglers and is a method of joining two lines. A knot quickly made, and is easy to undo, the ends being simply pulled apart.

8. MIDDLEMAN'S KNOT. To form this knot make two half hitches, one left handed and one right handed. Lay the two half hitches together, placing the right-hand loop on top of the left-hand one. Hold them together with the thumb of the left hand on top. Bring up the bight behind the hitches through the loops of the hitches. Tighten the hitches round the bight, being careful not to alter the position of the hitches.

WHIPPING

Loop the whipping twine and lay it alongside the end of the rope. Take the running end B round the rope about an inch and a half from the end. Now continue to bind the running end B round the rope end and the loop.

When you have got to about a quarter of an inch from the end of the rope, slip the running end B through the loop that lies alongside the rope. Now cut off the running end B about two inches from the loop, then pull on the standing end A. This will draw the loop, and at the same time the running end B, into the binding.

Trim the two ends A and B close to the complete whipping. Remember when making the turns to bind tightly.

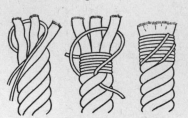

SAILMAKER'S WHIPPING

This is a very neat way of whipping the end of a rope, and is also quite secure provided you do it carefully and tightly. The drawings make the method clear.

Knots want a lot of practice as you soon forget them. Use pieces of rope or cord and not messy bits of string or bootlaces.

To prevent the end of a rope becoming frayed and unlaid you should whip the end of it. This is done by wrapping thin string round it several times and finishing it off so that the ends do not show. There are several methods of doing this and the picture shows an easy and efficient way.

We had no rope with us in West Africa, so we used the strong creeping plants, and also used thin withes or long whippy sticks, which we made still more pliant or bendable by holding one end under foot and twisting the other round and round with our hands.

The best wood for withes in England is willow or hazel. You see them used for binding faggots of wood together. You cannot tie all knots with them, as with rope, but you can generally make a timber hitch.

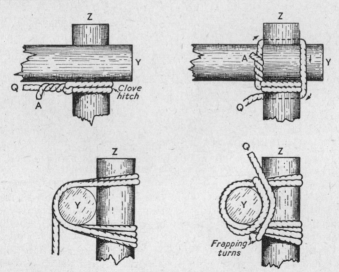

SQUARE LASHING

Begin with clove hitch under horizontal spar; follow round as shown by direction of arrows; pull tight at each stage; pack turns together neatly without crossing. After several complete turns, frapping turns (at right angles to main lashing) are made: these must be very tight. Finish off with clove hitch round handiest spar, keeping clove hitch at right angles to last turn. Go slowly, and keep all tight and firm.

Hut Building

To live comfortably in camp a Scout must know how to make a bivouac shelter for the night, or a hut if he is going to be for a long time in camp.

It all depends on the country and weather as to what sort of shelter you put up.

In making your roof—whether of branches of fir trees, or of grass or reeds, etc.—put them on as you would do tiles or slates, beginning at the bottom, so that the upper overlap the lower ones, and thus run off the rain without letting it through.

Notice which direction the wind generally blows from, and put the back of your shelter that way, with your fire in front of it.

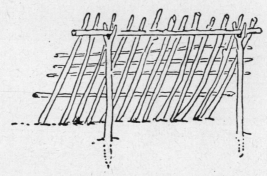

FRAMEWORK OF A BIVOUAC SHELTER

To be thatched with brushwood or grass. A second lean-to-roof on opposite side of ridge-pole will then make a hut.

The simplest shelter is to plant two forked sticks firmly in the ground, and rest a crossbar on them as ridge pole. Then lean other poles against it, or a hurdle or branches, and thatch it with grass, etc.

Or another good way, and quicker, is to cut one pole only and lean it against a tree, binding its end there; then thatch it with branches of brushwood, etc.

Where you have no poles available you can do as the South African natives do—pile up a lot of brushwood, heather, etc., into a small wall made in semi-circle to keep out the cold wind, and make your fire in the open part.

If your tent or hut is too hot in the sun, put blankets or more straw, etc., over the top. The thicker the roof the cooler is the tent in summer. If it is too cold, make the bottom of the walls thicker, or build a small wall of sods about a foot high round the foot of the wall outside. Never forget to dig a good drain all round your hut, so that if heavy rain comes in the night your floor will not get flooded from outside.

Zulus make their huts by planting in the ground a circle of long whippy sticks standing upright, then they bend the tops all down

AN EASILY-MADE HUT

towards the centre and tie them together, afterwards weaving whippy sticks round in and out of the uprights horizontally, until they have made a kind of circular bird-cage; this they then cover with a straw mat or thatch, or with straw woven into the sticks. Sometimes a small hole is left at the top where all the sticks join to act as a chimney.

The Red Indians make their "Tee Pee" with several poles tied together in the form of a pyramid, and over these they pass a piece of canvas, which at a little distance looks like a bell-tent.

Felling Trees

A Scout must know how to use an axe or bill-hook for chopping down small trees and branches.

The way to cut down a tree is first to chop out a chunk of wood near the bottom of the stem on that side to which you want the tree to fall, then go round to the other side, and chop away on the

First cut

HOW TO FELL
A TREE

opposite side of the stem an inch or two above the first cut until the tree topples over. It is a matter of practice to become a woodcutter, but you have to be very careful at first lest in chopping you miss the tree, and chop your own leg.

Never play the fool with an axe; it is a dangerous weapon, and when not in use should be kept masked. Before you start felling a tree make sure that your axe will not touch any branch or twig as in its swing it might be deflected and injure someone. Also make sure that onlookers are well away from you.

When the tree starts to fall shout out "Timber" as a warning, and take care not to stand behind the tree, as its top branches may catch on another tree and make the butt fly backwards.

How to Make Bridges

As I told you before, my scouts in Ashanti, when also acting as pioneers, had to build nearly two hundred bridges—and they had to make them out of any kind of material that they could find on the spot.

There are many ways of making bridges. In the Army they are generally made of poles lashed together. In India, in the Hima-

ROPE BRIDGE

laya mountains, the natives make bridges out of three ropes stretched across the river and connected together every few yards by V-shaped sticks, so that one rope forms the footpath and the other two make the handrail on each side. They are jumpy kind of bridges to walk across, but they take you over; and they are easily made.

The simplest way of bridging a narrow, deep stream is to fell a tree, or two trees side by side, on the bank, so that they fall across the stream. With an adze you then flatten the top side, put up a handrail and there you have a very good bridge.

Rafts, too, can be used. You build your raft alongside the bank, in the water if the river is shallow; on the bank if deep. When it is finished you hold on to the down-stream end, push the other out from the bank, and let the stream carry it down into position.

Self Measures

Every pioneer should know his exact personal measurement in the following details (of which I give the average man's measure):

Nail joint of forefinger, or breadth of thumb . .	1 inch
Span of thumb and forefinger	8 inches
Span of thumb and little finger or other finger .	9 inches
Wrist to elbow	10 inches
(This also gives you the length of your foot.)	
Elbow to tip of forefinger (called "cubit") . .	17 inches
Middle of kneecap to ground	18 inches

Extended arms, from finger-tip to finger-tip, is called a fathom, and nearly equals your height.

Pulse beats about 75 times a minute; each beat is a little quicker than a second.

Pace: A pace is about $2\frac{1}{2}$ feet; about 120 paces equal 100 yards. Fast walking paces are shorter than when going slow.

Fast walking you walk a mile in 16 minutes, or nearly four miles an hour.

Judging Heights and Distances

Every Scout must be able to judge distance from an inch up to a mile or more. You ought, first of all, to know exactly what is the span of your hand and the breadth of your thumb, and the length from your elbow to your wrist, and the length from one hand to the other with your arms stretched out to either side, and also the length of your feet; if you remember these accurately they are a great help to you in measuring things. Also it is useful to cut notches on your staff, showing such measurements as one inch, six inches, one foot and one yard. These you can measure off with a tape measure before you use your staff, and they may come in very useful..

Judging the distance of objects from you is only gained by practice, and judging the distance of a journey is generally estimated by seeing how long you have been travelling, and at what rate; that is to say, supposing you walk at the rate of four miles an hour, if you have been walking for an hour and a half you know that you have done about six miles.

Distance can also be judged by sound. That is to say, if you see a gun fired in the distance, and you count the number of seconds between the flash and the sound of the explosion reaching you, you will be able to tell how far off you are from the gun.

Sounds travels at the rate of 365 yards per second. That is, as many yards as there are days in the year.

A Scout must also be able to estimate heights, from a few inches up to three thousand feet or more; that is to say, he ought to be able to judge the height of a fence, the depth of a ditch, or the height of an embankment, of a house, tree, tower, hill, or mountain. It is easy to do when once you have practised it for a few times but it is very difficult to teach it by book.

You must also know how to estimate weights—a letter of an ounce, or a fish, or a potato of one pound, or a sack of bran, or a cartload of coals; and also the probable weight of a man from his appearance—these, again, are only learnt by practice, but as a Scout you should take care to learn them for yourself.

Also you should be able to judge numbers; that is to say, you should be able to tell at a glance *about* how many people are in a group, or on a 'bus, or in a big crowd, how many sheep in a flock, how many marbles on a tray, and so on. These you can practise for yourself at all times in the street or field.

Test the following from your own observations: —

At fifty yards, mouth and eyes of a man can be clearly seen.

At 100 yards, eyes appear as dots; 200 yards, buttons and details of clothes can still be seen; at 300 yards, face can be seen; at 400 yards, the movement of the legs can be seen; at 500 yards, the colour of clothes can be seen.

For distances over these, think out for yourself which point is half-way to the object. Estimate how far this may be from you, and then double it to obtain the distance. Or another way is to estimate the farthest distance that the object can be away, and then the very nearest it could be, and strike a mean between the two.

Objects appear nearer than they really are: First, when the light is bright and shining on the object; secondly, when looking across water or snow, or looking uphill or down. Objects appear farther off when in the shade; across a valley; when the background is of the same colour; when the observer is lying down or kneeling; when there is a heat haze over the ground.

Distance Across a River

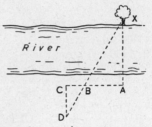

The way to estimate the distance across a river is to take an object X, such as a tree or rock on the opposite bank; start off at right angles to it from A, and pace, say, ninety yards along your bank; on arriving at sixty yards, plant a stick or stone, B; on arriving at C, thirty yards beyond that, that is ninety from the start, turn at right angles and walk inland, counting your paces until you bring the stick and the distant tree in line; the number of paces that you have taken from the bank C D will then give you the half distance across A X.

Height

To find the height of an object, such as a tree or house, pace a distance of eleven feet or yards or any unit you like and set up a staff with another Scout to hold it. Now pace one more unit of your chosen measurement, making twelve in all. Get your eye down to ground level at this spot and look up at the tree. The second Scout then slides his hand up or down the staff until your eye, his hand, and the top of the tree are all in line. Measure the distance in inches along the staff from the ground to the Scout's hand, call these inches feet, and that is the height of the object in feet. You can use any unit of measurement you find suitable as long as you make it eleven to one and you call inches feet on the staff.

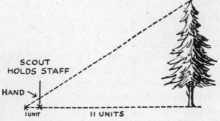

SCOUT
HOLDS STAFF

HAND

I UNIT   II UNITS

CAMP FIRE YARN. No. 9

CAMPING

Comfort in Camp

SOME people talk of "roughing" it in camp. Those people are generally "tenderfoots"; an old backwoodsman doesn't rough it, he knows how to look after himself, and to make himself comfortable by a hundred little dodges. For instance, if there are no tents he doesn't sit down to shiver and grouse, but at once sets to work to rig up a shelter or hut for himself. He chooses a good spot for it, where he is not likely to be flooded out if a storm of rain were to come on. Then he lights up a camp fire, and makes himself a comfortable mattress of ferns or straw. An old Scout is full of resource, that is, he can find a way out of any difficulty or discomfort.

Ground

In the first place you must think where you will have your camp, and what kind of camp it shall be.

The nearer you have it to your homes, the less will be the expense of travelling to and from camp.

The best place to my mind for a camp is in or close by a wood where you have leave to cut firewood and to build huts. So if you know of an owner in your neighbourhood who is likely to give you leave to use a corner of his wood, there is your chance. Inside, a wood is apt to be damp and to suffer from drip in wet weather, so you must be on the look-out for this. If you build good rain-proof huts, you need not have tents.

The seaside also gives some good camp grounds if you get a place where boats are available and bathing possible. Sometimes you can get the use of a boatshed or the cabin of a disused vessel to live in. Don't forget that you will want good water and some firewood.

Or you can go to mountains, moor, or river, and get leave to pitch your camp. But in choosing the site, always think what it would be if the weather came on very rainy and windy, and get the driest and most sheltered place you can and not too far away from your water supply, and remember that a good water supply is the first consideration. You must make quite sure that the water you are to drink is pure and you will find that you will not want to carry it very far.

Tramping Camps

Instead of a fixed camp, many Scouts prefer a "tramping camp."

Of course, it is much better fun to go over new country; but to make a tramping camp enjoyable you want good weather.

In arranging your tramp, your first point will be to select the line of country you want to visit, and mark out from the map whereabouts you will halt for each night. You will find that about five miles a day is as much as you will want to do.

You would do well to make a trek-cart for carrying your tents, blankets, and waterproof sheets, etc. At the end of each day's march you would get leave from a farmer to pitch your camp in his field, or to get the use of his barn to sleep in—especially if the weather be wet.

Boat Cruising

Another enjoyable way of camping is to take a boat and explore a river, camping out in the same way as in a tramping camp. But in this case every member of the Patrol must be able to swim.

One of the Rules says: No Scout shall take part in any boat training until he can swim fifty yards with clothes on (shirt, shorts, and socks as a minimum).

It is often very convenient to make your tent inside the boat at night.

Tents

Before you know which type of tent you will want, you must decide whether it will be wanted for a standing or moving camp.

For a standing camp, from which you don't mean to move, the best tent is the kind used by explorers called a ridge tent. They are rather expensive, but are unequalled for comfort and for making the camp look nice. If they have fly-sheets they will be quite waterproof, even if you touch the inside of the tent, and the fly-sheet will keep the tent cool in hot sunshine and warm in frosty weather.

Small Scout tents also do very well for camp if you can have two for each Patrol, and you can also make your own tents during the winter months—and this, perhaps, is the best way of all, as it comes cheapest in the end. And if, while you are about it, you make one or two extra ones, you may be able to sell them at a good profit.

Camp Equipment

When you have decided what kind of camp you intend to have, and whereabouts, your next point is to look to the equipment—that is to say, what you will need in the way of buckets, brooms,

tools, and so on. Here is a rough list of things that are useful in a standing camp, but they will not all be necessary in a bivouac or shifting camp.

FOR EACH PATROL:

Tent, with mallet and pegs.
Patrol flag.
Lantern (candle) and matches.
Wash bowl.
Hand axe.
Canvas for cooking shelter and dining shelter, with poles.
Three dixies.
Frying pan.
Roast bowl.
Two water buckets (one marked "Drinking water").
Milk jug.
Wooden spoon.

Kitchen knife and fork.
Mop.
Scrubbers.
Dish cloths and drying cloths.
Ladle.
Two large enamel serving plates.
Tin-opener.
Butter muslin.
Pudding cloth.

FOR EACH SCOUT:

Complete Scout uniform
Two blankets, or sleeping-bag.
Pyjamas or change for night.
Sweater.
Spare shirt and shorts, and stockings.
Spare boots or shoes.
Plimsolls or sandals.
Bathing trunks.
Towel.
Soap, comb, brush, toothbrush, etc., in toilet bag.
Handkerchiefs.
Mending materials.
Mackintosh.
Two enamelled soup plates.
Enamelled half-pint mug.
Knife, fork, spoon, in bag.
Groundsheet.
(Packed in) Rucsac or kit-bag, marked with name.

FOOD.—Food is often a difficulty. Though it may seem strange to a tenderfoot, Scouts know that neither bread nor meat is wholly necessary to keep them fit. Personally I very seldom eat either. Biscuits are good for camp food, and can be carried in your pocket or haversack, for which bread is useless.

The best kind of bread for camp is what the Boers and most South African hunters use, and that is "rusks." Rusks are easily made. You buy a stale loaf at the baker's at half-price, cut it up into thick slices or square "junks," and then bake these in an oven or toast them before a hot fire till they are quite hard like biscuits. They can then be carried in a spare haversack or bag, and do very well instead of bread. Soft bread easily gets damp and sour and stale in camp.

If fresh meat is used, be sure that it is *fresh*, and remember that eggs, rice, and porridge are easier to keep, and are just as good food. Fruit is easy to stew and good to eat. Cakes of chocolate are very useful in camp and on the march. I have often gone a whole day on an Army biscuit and a cake of chocolate.

Pitching Camp

Having chosen the spot for your camp, pitch your tent with the door away from the wind If heavy rain comes on dig a small trench about three inches deep all round it to prevent it getting

flooded. This trench should lead the water away downhill. Dig a small hole the size of a tea-cup alongside the foot of the pole into which to shift it if rain comes on. This enables you to slack up all ropes at once to allow for their shrinking when wet.

In Scouts' camps the tents are not pitched in lines and streets as in military camps, but are dotted about, fifty or a hundred yards apart or more, in a big circle round the Scoutmaster's tent, which, with the flag and camp fire, is generally in the centre. This keeps each Patrol separate as a unit.

WATER SUPPLY.—If there is a spring or stream, the best part of it must be strictly kept clear and clean for drinking water. Further downstream, a place may be appointed for bathing, washing clothes, and so on. The greatest care is always taken by Scouts to keep their drinking water supply very clean, otherwise they are very likely to get sickness among them.

All water has a large number of tiny animals floating about in it, too small to be seen without the help of a microscope. Some of them are poisonous, some are not; you can't tell whether the poisonous ones are there, so the safest way is to kill them all before you drink any water; and the way to kill them is to boil the water, and let it cool again before drinking it. In boiling the water don't let it merely come to a boil and then take it off, but let it boil fully for a quarter of an hour, as these little beasts, or microbes as they are called, are very tough customers, and take a lot of boiling before they are killed.

KITCHENS.—The cooking fire is made to leeward, or downwind of the camp, so that the smoke and sparks from the fire don't blow into the tents. Cooking fires are described on p. 78.

Old scouts always take special care to keep the kitchen particularly clean, as, if scraps are left lying about, flies collect and smells arise which are very likely to poison slightly the food while 'it is being got ready for a meal, and this brings sickness to the scouts. So keep the camp-kitchen and ground round it very clean at all times.

To do this you will want a wet and a dry pit. These are holes about eighteen inches square and a foot deep. The top of the wet one is covered with a layer of straw or grass and all wet refuse and greasy water is poured through this into the pit. The covering will collect the grease in the water and prevent it from clogging up the ground. The straw or grass should be burnt every day and renewed.

Into the dry pit is put everything else that will not burn. Tins and so on should be burnt first and then hammered out flat before being put in the dry pit. Burn everything you can or your pit will very soon be full. The rubbish should be covered with a layer of earth every evening.

LATRINES.—Another very important point for the health of the Scouts is to dig a trench to serve as a latrine. Before pitching tents or lighting the camp fire the latrines should be dug and screens erected. On reaching the camping-ground the latrines are the very first things to attend to—and all Scouts bear this in mind. The trench should be one foot deep, one foot wide, and three feet long, so that the user can squat astride of it, one foot on each side. A thick sprinkling of earth should be thrown in after use, and the whole trench carefully filled in with earth after a few days' use. The cross screens are necessary for decency, about which Scouts are always very careful.

There should also be a wet latrine made by digging a hole and half-filling it with stones for drainage.

Even in a one-night camp, Scouts should dig a latrine trench. And when rearing away from camp a Scout will always dig a small pit of a few inches, which he will fill in again after use.

Neglect of this not only makes a place unhealthy, but also it makes farmers and landowners disinclined to give the use of their ground for Scouts to camp on or to work over. So don't forget it, Scouts.

Bathing

When in camp, bathing will be one of your joys and one of your duties, a joy because it is such fun, a duty because no Scout can consider himself a full-blown Scout until he is able to swim and to save life in the water. But there are dangers about bathing for which every sensible Scout will be prepared.

First, there is the danger of cramp. This comes very often from staying in the water too long. Ten minutes is ample time as a rule for a boy to be in the water, five minutes is safer.

If you bathe within an hour and a half of taking a meal, that is before your food is digested, you are very likely to get cramp. Cramp doubles you up in extreme pain so that you cannot move your arms or legs, and down you go and drown—and it will be your own fault.

There should always be a bathing picket posted, while bathing is going on, of two good swimmers, who will not bathe themselves but will be ready undressed, except for overcoats, and prepared to jump in at any moment and help a bather if he is in difficulties. The picket himself should not bathe until the others have left the water, and a life line must be available.

Many lives are lost every summer through foolishness on the part of boys bathing because they don't think of these things. Bathing must only be permitted in safe places and under strict supervision.

Cleaning Camp Ground

Never forget also that the state of an old camp ground, after the camp has finished, tells exactly whether the Patrol or Troop which has used it was a smart one or not. No Scouts who are any good ever leave a camp ground dirty; they sweep up and bury or burn every scrap of rubbish. This is done on service to prevent the enemy reading any information from what is left.

Thus, supposing you left some bits of old bandages, a few tunic buttons, old food scraps, etc., an enemy could tell which regiments were in the force, that there were wounded men, and that the men were reduced to certain shifts for food.

In peace camps, it is quite as important to get into this habit of cleaning up your camp ground before leaving it, as then farmers don't have the trouble of having to clean their ground after you leave, and they are, therefore, all the more willing to let you use it again.

Remember, it is a big disgrace against any Troop or Patrol or lone camper if the camp ground is left dirty and untidy. The members of the Camping Club are wonderful in leaving no trace behind them that there has been a camp. I have even seen them brushing the grass with a clothes' brush to make it stand up again where they had been lying. And I've been glad to see Scouts doing the same. Remember also the two things you leave behind you on breaking up camp:

1. Nothing.
2. Your thanks to the owner of the ground.

I have more than once found nice totem sticks left standing in my field when Scouts have been camping there with Morse writing or Indian signs giving me their thanks.

Payment

Another point to remember is that when you use a farmer's ground you ought to repay him for the use of it. If you do not do this with money you can do it in other ways. You can, and ought to do, jobs that are useful for him. You can mend his fences or gates, or herd his cows, cut thistles or dig up weeds, and so on. You should always be doing " good turns " both to the farmer and to the people living near your camp, so that they will be glad to have you there.

Trespassing

Especially be careful to get leave from the owners of land in the neighbourhood before you go on to it. You have no right to go anywhere off the roads without leave, but most owners will give you this if you go and tell them who you are and what you want to do.

When going over their land remember above all things:

1. Leave all gates as you found them.
2. Disturb animals and game as little as you possibly can.
3. Do no damage to fences, crops, or trees.

Any firewood that you require you must ask for before taking, and be careful not to take out of hedges dead wood which is being used to fill up a gap.

Loafers in Camp

A camp is a roomy place, but there is no room in it for one chap, and that is the fellow who does not want to take his share in the many little odd jobs that have to be done; there is no room for the shirker or the *grouser*—well, there is no room for them in the Boy Scouts at all, but least of all when in camp.

Every fellow must help, and help cheerily, in making it comfortable for all. In this way comradeship grows. On service, if one fellow is out on night duty getting wet through, one of those left in the tent will be sure to get ready a cup of hot cocoa for him when he comes in, and that is the kind of thing every Scout should think of and carry out.

Camp Beds

There are many ways of making a comfortable bed in camp, but always have a rubber waterproof sheet over the ground between your body and the earth. Cut-grass or straw or bracken is a very good thing to lay down thickly where you are going to lie, but if you cannot get any of these and are obliged to lie on the ground, do not forget before lying down to make a small hole about the size of a teacup in which your hip joint will rest when you are lying on your side; it makes all the difference in sleeping comfortably. A very comfortable bed, almost a spring mattress, is made in Canada by cutting a large number of tops of the fir-tree branches, and planting them upright in the ground as close together as possible, like bristles in a brush, so close that when you lie down on them they form a comfortable and springy couch.

Remember, when sleeping in camp the secret of keeping warm is to have as many blankets *underneath* you as you have above you. If a Patrol were sleeping round a fire, you would all lie with your feet towards it like the spokes of a wheel. If your blankets do not keep you sufficiently warm, put straw or bracken over yourselves, and newspapers, if you have them. It is also a good tip in cold weather, if you have not sufficiently warm clothing, to put a newspaper under your coat or waistcoat up your back and round your body; it will be as good as an overcoat in giving you extra warmth.

To make a bed, cut four poles—two of seven feet, two of three —lay them on the ground, so as to form the edges.

Cut eight pegs, two feet long, sharpen, and drive them into the ground at the four corners to keep the poles in place.

Cut down a fir tree, cut off all branches and lay them overlapping each other like slates on a roof till a thick bed of them is made; the outside ones underlapping the poles. Cover with a blanket.

To make a mattress, you first set up a camp loom (as described at the end of this yarn), and weave a mattress out of bracken,

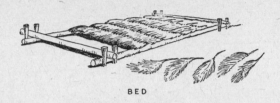

BED

ferns, heather, straw, or grass, etc., six feet long, and two feet nine inches across.

With this same loom you can make grass or straw mats, with which to form tents, or shelters, or walls, or carpets, etc.

Camp candlesticks can be made by bending a bit of wire into a small spiral spring; or by using a cleft stick stuck in the wall; or by sticking the candle upright in a lump of clay or in a hole bored in a big potato; or a glass candle shade can be made by cutting the bottom off a bottle, and sticking it upside down in the ground with a candle stuck in the neck.

The bottom of the bottle may be cut off, either by putting about an inch or an inch and a half of water into the bottle, and then standing it in the embers of the fire till it gets hot and cracks at the water-level. Or it can be done by passing a piece of string round the body of the bottle, and drawing it rapidly to and fro till it makes a hot line round the bottle, which then breaks neatly off with a blow, or on being immersed in cold water, but remember that cut glass and cut tins are dangerous things in camp.

Camp forks can also be made out of wire sharpened at the points.

It is something to know how to sit down in a wet camp. You "squat" instead of sitting. Natives in India squat on their heels, but this is a tiring way if you have not done it as a child; though it comes easy if you put a sloping stone or chock of wood under

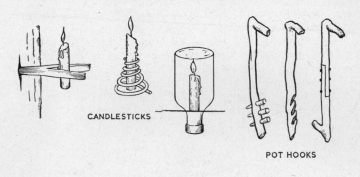

CANDLESTICKS

POT HOOKS

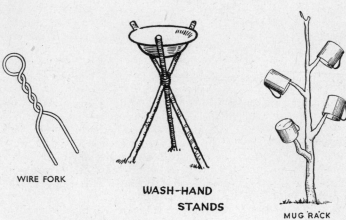

WIRE FORK

WASH-HAND
STANDS

MUG RACK

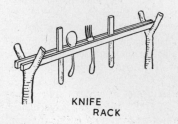

KNIFE
RACK

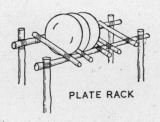

PLATE RACK

CAMP FURNITURE

your heels. Boers and other camp men squat on one heel. It is a little tiring at first.

A great secret of sleeping comfortably in camp is to have a canvas bag about two feet long by one foot wide, into which you

pack odds and ends—or carry empty, and fill up with grass or underclothing to form your pillow at night.

Camp Fires—The Right Way of Making Them

Before lighting your fire, remember always to do as every backwoodsman does, and that is to cut away or burn all bracken, heather, grass, etc., round the fire, to prevent its setting light to the surrounding grass or bush. Many bad bush-fires have been caused by young tenderfoots fooling about with blazes which they imagined to be camp fires. In burning the grass for this purpose (or "ring-burning," as it is called), burn only a little at a time, and have branches of trees or old sacks ready with which you can beat it out again at once when it has gone far enough.

Scouts should always be on the look-out to beat out a bush-fire that has been accidentally started at any time, as a "good-turn" to the owner of the land or to people who may have herds and crops in danger.

It is no use to learn how to light a fire by hearsay; the only way is to pay attention to the instructions given you, and then practise laying and lighting a fire yourself.

In the book called *Two Little Savages,* instructions for laying a fire are given in the following rhyme:

"First a curl of birch bark as dry as it can be,
Then some twigs of soft wood dead from off a tree,
Last of all some pine knots to make a kettle foam,
And there's a fire to make you think you're sitting right at home."

Remember to begin your fire with a small amount of very small chips or twigs of really dry dead wood lightly heaped together,

and a little straw or paper to ignite it; about this should be put
little sticks leaning together in the shape of a pyramid, and above
this bigger sticks similarly standing on end. When the fire is well
alight bigger sticks can be added, and finally logs of wood. A great
thing for a cooking fire is to get a good pile of red-hot wood ashes,
and if you use three large logs, they should be placed lying on the
ground, star-shaped, like the spokes of a wheel, with their ends
centred in the fire. A fire made in this way need never go out, for
as the logs burn away you keep pushing them towards the centre
of the fire, always making fresh red-hot ashes. This makes
a good cooking fire, and also one which gives very little flame or
smoke for the enemy to detect from a distance.

To keep your fire alight at night, cover it over with a heap of
ashes, and it will smoulder all night ready for early use in the
morning, when you can easily blow it into a glow.

If you want to keep a fire going all night to show or to warm
you, put good-sized logs end to end star-shaped—and one long
one reaching to your hand, so that you can push it in from time to
time to the centre without trouble of getting up to stoke the fire.

Tongs are useful about a camp fire, and can be made from a
rod of beech, or other tough wood, about four feet long and one
inch thick. Shave it away in the middle to about half its proper
thickness, and put this part into the hot embers of the fire for a
few moments, and bend the stick over till the two ends come together. Then flatten away the inside edges of the ends so that they
have a better grip—and there are your tongs.

A broom is also useful for keeping the camp clean, and can
easily be made with a few sprigs of birch bound tightly round a
stake.

STAR FIRE

CRANE

HUNTER OR
TRAPPER FIRE

Plan →

ROAST BOWL

BISCUIT-TIN
OVEN

REFLECTOR FIRE

CAMP FIRES AND KITCHENS

Drying Clothes

You often get wet through on service, and you will see tender-foots remaining in their wet clothes until they get dry again; no old scout would do so, as that is the way to catch fever and get ill. When you are wet, take the first opportunity of getting your wet clothes off and drying them, even though you may not have other clothes to put on, as happened to me many a time. I have sat naked under a waggon while my one suit of clothes was drying over a fire. The way to dry clothes over a fire is to make a fire of hot ashes, and then build a small beehive-shaped cage of sticks over the fire, and then to hang your clothes all over this cage, and they will very quickly dry. Also, in hot weather it is dangerous to sit in your clothes when they have got wet from your perspiration. On the West Coast of Africa I always carried a spare shirt, hanging down my back, with the sleeves tied round my neck; as soon as I halted I would take off the wet shirt I was wearing, and put on the dry, which had been hanging out in the sun on my back. By this means I never got fever when almost everyone else went down with it.

Tidiness

The camp ground should at all times be kept clean and tidy, not only (as I have pointed out) to keep flies away, but also because if you go away to another place, and leave an untidy ground behind you, it gives so much important information to enemy scouts. For this reason Scouts are always tidy, whether in camp or not, as a matter of habit. If you are not tidy at home, you won't be tidy in camp; and if you're not tidy in camp, you will be only a tenderfoot and no Scout.

A Scout is tidy also in his tent, bunk or room, because he may be suddenly called upon to go off on an alarm, or something unexpected; and if he does not know exactly where to lay his hand on his things, he will be a long time in turning out, especially if called up in the middle of the night. So on going to bed, even

SHOE LACED IN THE SCOUT'S WAY

when at home, practise the habit of folding up your clothes and putting them where you can at once find them in the dark, and get into them quickly.

A Scout even ties his shoe laces neatly—in fact, they are not tied, but are woven through the eyelet holes from top of the shoe downwards, and so need no tying.

The Camp Loom

Plant a row of five stakes 2 ft. 6 in. firmly in the ground; about 6 ft. or 7 ft. away from this row drive in another row of five or two corner ones with a crossbar joining them.

Fasten a cord to the head of each stake in the first row, stretch it to the corresponding stake in the other row or to the crossbar and make it fast on the stake or crossbar. Then carry the cord back to the first row, allow 5 ft. extra, cut the cord and tie the end to a loose "beam" or crossbar at exactly the same distances apart from the next cord as it is on the stakes.

This "beam" is then moved up and down by one Scout, while the remainder lay bundles of bracken, heather, fern or straw, etc., in layers alternately under and over the stretched cords.

If you move the beam first to the right and then to the left, so that the cords fastened to it pull first on one side and then on the other side of the stretched cords, it will twist them and make the binding more secure.

CAMP COOKING
Cooking

Every Scout must, of course, know how to cook his own meat and vegetables, and to make bread for himself, without regular cooking utensils. For boiling water a Scout would usually have his tin "billy," and in that he can boil vegetables or stew his meat; but often he will want it for drinking, and will cook his meat in some other way. This would usually be done by sticking it on sharp sticks and hanging it close to the fire, so that it gets broiled; or the lid of an old biscuit tin can be used as a kind of frying-pan. Put grease or water in it to prevent the meat getting burnt before it is cooked.

Meat can also be wrapped in a few sheets of wet paper, or in a coating of clay, and put in the red-hot embers of the fire, where it will cook itself. Birds and fish can also be cooked in this manner, and there is no need to pluck the bird before doing so if you use clay, as the feathers will stick to the clay when it hardens in the heat, and when you break it open the bird will come out cooked, without its feathers, like the kernel out of a nutshell.

Another way is to clean out the inside of the bird, get a pebble about the size of its inside, and heat it till nearly red-hot; place it inside the bird, and put the bird on a gridiron, or on a wooden spit over the fire.

Birds are most easily plucked immediately after being killed.

Don't do as I did once when I was a tenderfoot. It was my turn to cook, so I thought I would vary the dinner by giving them soup. I had some pea-flour, and I mixed it with water and boiled it up, and served it as pea-soup; but I did not put in any stock or meat juice of any kind. I didn't know that it was necessary or would be noticeable. But they noticed it directly, called my beautiful soup a "wet pease-pudding," and told me I might eat it myself—not only told me I *might,* but they jolly well *made* me eat it. I never made the mistake again.

To boil your "billy," or camp kettle, you can either stand it on the logs (where it often falls over unless care is taken), or, better, stand it on the ground among the hot embers of the fire; or else rig up a triangle of three green poles over the fire, tying them together at the top, and hanging the pot by a wire or chain from the poles. But in making this tripod do not, if there is an old scout in camp, use poplar sticks for poles, because, although they are easy to cut and trim for the purpose, old-fashioned scouts have a fancy that they bring bad luck to the cooking. Any other kind of wood will do better.

As good a kind of camp kitchen as any is made with two lines of sods, bricks, thick logs or stones, flattened at the top, about six feet long, slightly splayed from each other, being four inches apart at one end and eight inches at the other—the big end towards the wind.

Another way, when there are several "billies" to cook, is to put them in two lines a few inches apart, one end of the line facing towards the wind. Lay your fire of small wood between the two lines, and put a third row of "billies" standing on top of the first two rows—so that a small tunnel is made by the "billies." In the windward end of this tunnel start your fire; the draught will carry its heat along the tunnel, and this will heat all the pots. The fire should be kept up with small split chunks of wood.

When boiling a pot of water on the fire, do not jam the lid on too firmly, as, when the steam forms inside the pot, it must have some means of escape or it will burst the pot.

To find out when the water is beginning to boil, you need not take off the lid and look, but just hold the end of a stick or knife, etc., to the pot, and if the water is boiling you will feel it trembling.

Kabobs.—Cut your meat up into a slice about half or three-quarters of an inch thick; cut this up into small pieces about one to one and a half inches across. String a lot of these chunks on to a stick or iron rod, and plant it in front of the fire, or suspend it over the hot embers for a few minutes till the meat is roasted.

Hunter's Stew.—Cut some lean meat or game into small pieces, brown it with fat in a frying-pan, shuffling the pan so as to sear but not burn the surface of the meat. Then drop the meat into a kettle of boiling water and set it to one side or hang it high

over the fire so as to simmer. Later add potatoes, onions, rice and
salt and pepper. It is essential that the water should not boil hard,
but merely simmer after the meat and vegetables are put in. The
time varies according to the materials used; cook until tender.
Do not use any fat meat.

If a thick stew is desired, rub up a little flour into the grease
left in the frying-pan, and add water, stir, and let the mixture boil
a little, then stir this thickening into the stew a short time before
it is ready.

Almost any meat, vegetable and cereal can be used in the stew.

Hay-box Cooking

This is the best way of getting your cooking done in camp, as
you only have to start it and the hay-box does the rest. You can
then go out and play your camp games with the other fellows, and
come back to find your dinner has cooked itself—that is, if you
started it right. If you didn't—well, you won't find yourself very
popular with the Troop!

This is how you should start it. Get a wooden box such as a
sugar box. Line it with several thicknesses of newspaper at sides
and bottom, then fill it with hay or more newspapers; pack this
all tight with a space in the middle for your cooking pot. Plenty
of hay below as well as round the pot. Make a cushion packed
with hay to form the top, or a thick pad of folded newspapers.

Get your stewpot full of food, and as soon as it is well on the
boil pop it into the hay-box. Pack the hay or paper *tight round*
it and over it, put on the covering pad, and jam down the lid with
a weight on it.

Meat will take four or five hours to cook in this way. Porridge
about two hours. Oatmeal you should boil for five minutes, and
leave in hay-box all night. It will be ready for your early breakfast.

Bread-making

"The three Bs of life in camp are bannocks, beans and bacon—
and the ability to cook them."

To make bread, or bannocks, the usual way is to make a pile of
flour and scoop out the centre until it forms a cup for the water,
which is then poured in; then mix the dough with a pinch or two
of salt and of baking powder, and knead and mix it well together
until it forms a lump of well-mixed dough. Then, with a little
fresh flour sprinkled over the hands to prevent the dough sticking
to them, pat it and make it into the shape of a large bun or several
buns. Then the Scout puts it on a gridiron over hot ashes, or

sweeps part of the fire to one side, and on the hot ground left there he puts his dough, and piles hot ashes round it and lets it bake itself. Only small loaves, or bannocks, like buns, can be made in this way.

If real bread is required a kind of oven has to be made, either by using an old earthenware pot or tin box, and putting it into the fire and piling fire all over it, or by making a clay oven, lighting a fire inside it, and then, when it is well heated, raking out the fire and putting the dough inside, and shutting up the entrance tightly till the bread is baked.

Another way is to cut a stout club, sharpen its thin end, peel it, and heat it in the fire. Make a long strip of dough, about two inches wide and half an inch thick: wind it spirally down the club; then plant the club close to the fire and let the dough toast itself, just giving the club a turn now and then. This is called a twist.

Cleanliness

One thing to remember in camp is that if you get sick you are no use as a Scout, and are only a burden to others, and you generally get ill through your own fault. Either you don't change into dry clothes when you get wet, or you let dirt get into your food, or you drink bad water.

So, when cooking your food, always be careful to clean your cooking pots, plates, forks, etc., very thoroughly.

Flies are most dangerous, because they carry about seeds of disease on their feet, and if they settle on your food they will often leave the poison there for you to eat—and then you wonder why you get ill. Flies generally live best where dirt and scraps of food are left lying about.

For this reason you should be careful to keep your camp very clean, so that flies won't come there. All slops and scraps should be thrown away into a properly dug hole, where they can be buried, and not scattered about all over the place. Patrol Leaders must be very careful to see that this is always done.

For the same reason, it is very dangerous to drink out of streams, and especially out of ponds, when you feel thirsty, for you may suck down any amount of poison in doing so. If a pond is your only water-supply, it is best to dig a small well, three feet deep, about ten feet away from the pond, and the water will ooze through into it, and will be much more healthy to drink.

We did this in Mafeking when the Boers cut off our regular water-supply, and so had no sickness from bad water.

CAMP FIRE YARN. No. 11

OBSERVATION OF "SIGN"

Noticing "Sign"

"SIGN" is the word used by scouts to mean any little details, such as footprints, broken twigs, trampled grass, scraps of food, a drop of blood, a hair, and so on; anything that may help as clues in getting the information they are in search of.

A lady, when travelling in Kashmir, was following up with some native Indian trackers the "pugs" of a panther which had killed and carried off a young buck. He had crossed a wide bare slab of rock which, of course, gave no mark of his soft feet. The tracker went at once to the far side of the rock where it came to a sharp edge; he wetted his finger, and just passed it along the edge till he found a few buck's hairs sticking to it. This showed him where the panther had passed down off the rock, dragging the buck with him. Those few hairs were what scouts call "sign."

This tracker also found bears by noticing small "sign." On one occasion he noticed a fresh scratch in the bark of a tree evidently made by a bear's claw, and on another he found a single black hair sticking to the bark of a tree, which told him that a bear had rubbed against it.

One of the most important things that a scout has to learn, whether he is a war scout or a hunter or peace scout, is *to let nothing escape his attention;* he must notice small points and signs, and then make out the meaning of them; but it takes a good deal of practice before a tenderfoot can get into the habit of really noting everything and letting nothing escape his eyes. It can be learnt just as well in a town as in the country.

And in the same way you should notice any strange sound or any peculiar smell and think for yourself what it may mean. Unless you learn to notice "sign" you will have very little of "this and that" to put together, and so you will be no use as a scout. It comes by practice.

Remember, a Scout always considers it a great disgrace if an outsider discovers a thing before he has seen it for himself, whether that thing is far away in the distance or close by under his feet.

If you go out with a really trained scout you will see that his eyes are constantly moving, looking out in every direction near and far, noticing everything that is going on, just from habit, not because he wants to show off how much he notices.

Once I was walking with one in Hyde Park in London. He presently remarked, "That horse is going a little lame"—there was no horse near us, but I found he was looking at one far away across the Serpentine: the next moment he picked up a peculiar button lying by the path. His eyes, you see, were looking both far away and near.

In the streets of a strange town a Scout will notice his way by the principal buildings and side-streets, and in any case he will notice what shops he passes and what is in their windows; also what vehicles pass him and such details as whether the horses' harness and shoes are all right; and most especially what people he passes, what their faces are like, their dress, their boots, and their way of walking, so that if, for instance, he should be asked by a policeman, "Have you seen a man with dark overhanging eyebrows, dressed in a blue suit, going down this street?" he should be able to give some such answer as "Yes—he was walking a little lame with the right foot, wore foreign-looking boots, was carrying a parcel in his hand, he turned down Gold Street, the second turning on the left from here, about three minutes ago."

Information of that kind has often been of the greatest value in tracing out a criminal, but so many people go along with their eyes shut and never notice things.

In the story of "Kim," by Rudyard Kipling, there is an account of two boys being taught "observation" in order to become detectives, or scouts, by means of a game in which a trayful of small objects was shown to them for a minute and was then covered over and they had to describe all the things on it from memory.

We have that game, as it is excellent practice for Scouts.

There was a revolutionary society in Italy called the Camorra, who used to train their boys to be quick at noticing and remembering things. When walking through the streets of the city, the Camorrist would suddenly stop and ask his boy—"How was the woman dressed who sat at the door of the fourth house on the right in the last street?" or "What were the two men talking about whom we met at the corner of the last street but three?" or, "Where was the cab ordered to drive to, and what was its number?" "What is the height of that house and what is the width of its upper-floor window?" and so on. Or the boy was given a minute to look in a shop window, and then he had to describe all that was in it. Captain Cook, the great explorer and scout, was trained in the same way as a boy, and so was Houdini, the great conjurer.

Every town Scout should know, as a matter of course, where is the nearest chemist's shop (in case of accidents), the nearest police "fixed point," police station, hospital, fire alarm, telephone, ambulance station, etc.

The Scout must also have his eyes on the ground, especially along the edge of the pavement against the houses or in the gutter. I have often found valuable trinkets that have been dropped, and which have been walked over by numbers of people, and kicked to one side without being noticed.

Details of People

When you are travelling by train or tram, always notice every little thing about your fellow-travellers; notice their faces, dress, way of talking, and so on, so that you could describe them each pretty accurately afterwards; and also try and make out from their appearance and behaviour whether they are rich or poor (which you can generally tell from their boots), and what is their probable business, whether they are happy, or ill, or in want of help.

But in doing this you must not let them see you are watching them, else it puts them on their guard. Remember the shepherd-boy who noticed the gipsy's boots, but did not look at him, and so did not make the gipsy suspicious of him.

Close observation of people and ability to read their character and their thoughts are of immense value in trade and commerce, especially for a shop-assistant or salesman in persuading people to buy goods, or in detecting would-be swindlers.

It is said that you can tell a man's character from the way he wears his hat. If it is slightly on one side, the wearer is good-natured; if it is worn very much on one side, he is a swaggerer; if on the back of his head, he is bad at paying his debts; if worn straight on the top, he is probably honest, but very dull.

The way a man (or a woman) walks is often a good guide to his character—witness the fussy, swaggering little man paddling along with short steps with much arm-action; the nervous man's hurried, jerky stride; the slow slouch of the loafer; the smooth, quick, and silent step of the scout, and so on.

Practise Observation

With a little practice in observation, you can tell pretty accurately a man's character from his dress.

I was speaking with a detective not long ago about a gentleman we had both been talking to, and we were trying to make out his character. I remarked, "Well, at any rate, he is a fisherman"; but my companion could not see why—but then he was not a fisherman himself. I had noticed a lot of little tufts of cloth sticking up on the left cuff of his coat.

(A good many fishermen, when they take their flies off the line, stick them into their cap to dry; others stick them into their sleeve. When dry they pull them out, which often tears a thread or two of the cloth.)

It is an amusing practice, when you are in a railway carriage or omnibus with other people, to look only at their feet and guess, without looking any higher, what sort of people they are, old or young, well-to-do or poor, fat or thin, and so on, and then look up and see how near you have been to the truth.

Remember how "Sherlock Holmes" met a stranger and noticed that he was looking fairly well-to-do, in new clothes with a mourning band on his sleeve, with a soldierly bearing, and a sailor's way of walking, sunburnt, with tattoo marks on his hands, and he was carrying some children's toys in his hand. What should you have supposed that man to be? Well, Sherlock Holmes guessed, correctly, that he had lately retired from the Royal Marines as a Sergeant, and his wife had died, and he had some small children at home.

It is through knowing how to observe people, without showing that they are doing so, that Boy Scouts can often get useful information.

Sign Round a Dead Body

It may happen to some of you that one day you will be the first to find the dead body of a man, in which case you will remember that it is your duty to examine and note down the smallest signs that are to be seen on and near the body before it is moved or the ground disturbed and trampled down. Besides noticing the exact position of the body (which should, if possible, be photographed exactly as found) the ground all round should be very carefully examined—without treading on it yourself more than is absolutely necessary, for fear of spoiling existing tracks. If you can also draw a little map of how the body lay and where the signs round it were, it might be of value.

Twice lately bodies have been found which were at first supposed to be those of people who had hanged themselves; but close examination of the ground round them—in one case some torn twigs and trampled grass, and in the other a crumpled carpet—showed that murder had been committed, and that the bodies had been hanged after death to make it appear as though they had committed suicide.

Finger-marks should especially be looked for on any likely articles, and if they do not correspond to those of the murdered man they may be those of his murderer, who could then be identified by comparing the impression with his fingers. Such a case occurred in India, where a man was found murdered and a bloody finger-mark on his clothes. The owner of the finger-mark was found, tried, and convicted.

There was the case of a learned old gentleman who was found dead in his bedroom with a wound in his forehead and another in his left temple.

Very often after a murder the murderer, with his hands bloody from the deed and running away, may catch hold of the door, or a jug of water to wash his hands.

In the present case a newspaper lying on the table had the marks of three blood-stained fingers on it. The son of the dead man was suspected and was arrested by the police.

But careful examination of the room and the prints of the finger-marks showed that the old gentleman had been taken ill in the night—had got out of bed to get some medicine, but getting near the table a new spasm seized him and he fell, striking his head violently against the corner of the table, and made the wound on his temple; which just fitted the corner. In trying to get up he had caught hold of the table and the newspaper on it and had made the bloody finger-marks on the newspaper in doing so. Then he had fallen again, cutting his head a second time on the foot of the bed.

The finger-marks were compared with the dead man's fingers, and were found to be exactly the same. Well, you don't find two men in 64,000,000,000,000 with the same pattern on the skin of their fingers. So it was evident there had been no murder, and the dead man's son was released as innocent.

In Leningrad, in Russia, a banker was found murdered. Near the body was found a cigar-holder with an amber mouthpiece. This mouthpiece was of peculiar shape and could only be held in the mouth in one position, and it had two teeth marks on it. These marks showed that the two teeth were of different lengths.

The teeth of the murdered man were quite regular, so the cigar-holder was evidently not his. But his nephew had teeth which corresponded to the marks on the mouthpiece, so he was arrested, and then further proof came up and showed that he was the murderer.

Details in the Country

If you are in the country you should notice landmarks, that is, objects which help you to find your way or prevent you getting lost, such as distant hills, church towers, and nearer objects, such as peculiar buildings, trees, gates, rocks, etc.

And remember in noticing such landmarks, that you may want to use your knowledge of them some day for telling someone else how to find his way, so you must notice them pretty closely so as to be able to describe them unmistakably and in their proper order. You must notice and *remember* every by-road and foot-path.

Then you must also notice smaller signs, such as birds getting up and flying hurriedly, which means somebody or some animal is there; dust shows animals, men, or vehicles moving.

Of course, when in the country you should notice just as much as in town all passers-by very carefully—how they are dressed, what their faces are like, and their way of walking, and examine their footmarks—and jot down a sketch of them in your note-book, so that you would know the footmark again if you found it somewhere else—(as the shepherd boy did in the story at the beginning of this book).

And notice all tracks—that is, footmarks of men, animals, birds, wheels, etc., for from these you can read the most important information. This track-reading is of such importance that I shall give you a yarn on that subject by itself.

Using your Eyes

Let nothing be too small for your notice; a button, a match, cigar ash, a feather, or a leaf, might be of great importance.

Remember, too, that there are a number of people now who wear the Scout's Thanks Badge, and it would be a great disgrace to a Scout if he let one of these people pass him without noticing it.

A Scout must not only look to his front, but also to either side and behind him; he must have "eyes at the back of his head," as the saying is. Often, by suddenly looking back, you will see an enemy's scout or a thief showing himself in a way that he would not have done had he thought you would look round.

Night Scouting

A Scout has to be able to notice small details just as much by night as by day, and this he has to do chiefly by listening, occasionally by feeling or smelling.

In the stillness of the night, sounds carry farther than by day. If you put your ear to the ground or place it against a stick, or especially against a drum, which is touching the ground, you will hear the shake of horses' hoofs or the thud of a man's footfall a long way off. Another way is to open a knife with a blade at each end, stick one blade into the ground and hold the other between your teeth and you will hear all the better. The human voice, even though talking low, carries to a great distance, and is not likely to be mistaken for any other sound.

I have often passed through outposts at night after having found where the pickets were posted by hearing the low talking of the men or the snoring of those asleep.

CAMP FIRE YARN. No. 12

SPOORING

Men's Tracks

GENERAL DODGE, of the American Army, described how he once had to pursue a party of Red Indians who had been murdering some people.

The murderers had nearly a week's start, and had gone away on horseback. But General Dodge got a splendid tracking-scout named Espinosa to help him. The Indians were all riding unshod horses, except one, and after Espinosa had been tracking them for many miles he suddenly got off his horse and pulled four horseshoes out of a hidden crevice in the rocks. The Indians had evidently pulled them off so that they should not leave a track.

For six days they pursued the band, and for a great part of the time there was no sign visible to an ordinary eye, and after going for 150 miles they eventually overtook and captured the whole party. But it was all entirely due to Espinosa's good tracking.

On another occasion some American troops were following up a number of Indians, who had been raiding and murdering whites, and they had some other Red Indian scouts to assist them in tracking. In order to make a successful track, they marched by night, and the trackers found the way in the darkness by feeling the tracks of the enemy with their hands, and they went at a fairly good pace for many miles, merely touching the track with their fingers; but suddenly they halted and reported that the track they had been following had been crossed by a fresh track, and on the commanding officer going up, he found the Indians still holding the track with their hands, so that there should be no mistake. A light was brought and it was found that the new track was that of a bear which had walked across the trail of the enemy! So the march continued without further incident, and the enemy were surprised, and caught in the early hours of the morning.

The Scout, Burnham, in South Africa, who was with Wilson's party when they were massacred on the Shanghani River in Matabeleland, was sent away with a dispatch shortly before they were surrounded. He travelled during the night to escape the observation of the enemy. He found his way by feeling for the tracks left in the mud by the column when it marched up there in the morning.

I myself led a column through an intricate part of the Matoppo

Hills in Rhodesia by night to attack the enemy's stronghold which I had reconnoitred the previous day. I found the way by feeling my own tracks, sometimes with my hands and sometimes through the soles of my shoes, which had worn very thin; and I never had any difficulty in finding the line.

Tracking, or following up tracks, is called by different names in different countries. Thus, in South Africa, you would talk only of "spooring," that is, following up the "spoor"; in India, it would be following the "pugs," or "pugging"; in America, it is "trailing."

It is one of the principal ways by which scouts gain information, and hunters find their game. But to become a good tracker you must begin young, and practise it at all times when you are out walking, whether in town or country.

If at first you constantly remind yourself to do it, you will soon find that you do it as a habit without having to remind yourself. And it is a very useful habit, and makes the dullest walk interesting.

Hunters when they are looking about in a country to find game first look for any tracks, old and new, to see if there are any animals in the country; then they study the newer marks to find out where the animals are hiding themselves; then, after they have found a fresh track, they follow it up till they find the animal and kill it; and afterwards they often have to retrace their own tracks to find their way back to camp. And war scouts do much the same as regards their enemies.

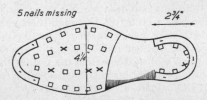

The way in which the diagram of a boot-track should be drawn.

First of all you must be able to distinguish one man's footmark from that of another, by its size, shape, and nails, etc. And, similarly, the prints of horses and other animals.

From a man's track, that is, from the size of his foot and the length of his stride, you can tell, to a certain extent, his height.

In taking notes of a track you should pick out a well-marked print, very carefully measure its length, length of heel, with widest point of tread, width at waist, width of heel, number of rows of nails, and number of nails in each row, heel and toe-plates or nails, shape of nail-heads, nails missing, etc.

It is best to make a diagram of the foot-print as shown.

You should also measure very carefully the length of the man's stride from the toe of one foot to the heel of the other.

A man was once found drowned in a river. It was supposed that he must have fallen in accidentally, and that the cuts on his head were caused by stones, etc., in the river. But someone took a drawing of his boots, and after searching the river-bank came on his tracks, and followed them up to a spot where there had evidently been a struggle, the ground being much trampled and bushes broken down to the water's edge, and the track of two other men's feet. And though these men were never found, it showed the case to be one of probable murder, which would not otherwise have been suspected.

A Scout must learn to recognise at a glance at what pace the maker of the tracks was going, and so on.

A man walking puts the whole flat of his foot on the ground, each foot a little under a yard from the other. In running, the toes are more deeply dug into the ground, and a little dirt is kicked up, and the feet are more than a yard apart. Sometimes men walk backwards in order to deceive anyone who may be tracking, but a good scout can generally tell this at once by the stride being shorter, the toes more turned in, and the heels being tightly impressed.

With animals, if they are moving fast, their toes are more deeply dug into the ground, and they kick up the dirt, and their paces are longer than when going slowly.

Wheel tracks should also be studied till you can tell the difference between the track of a lorry, a cart, motor-car or a bicycle, *and the direction they were going in.*

In addition to learning to recognise the pace of tracks, you must get to know how old they are. This is a most important point, and requires a very great amount of practice and experience before you can judge it really well.

So much depends on the state of the ground and weather, and its effects on the "spoor." If you follow one track, say, on a dry, windy day, over varying ground, you will find that when it is on light, sandy soil, it will look old in a very short time, because any

(1)

(2)

(2) *The direction of a bicycle is further shown by the loops made in the track where the rider has made a turn or wobble; the thinner end of the loop points in the direction he was going.*

(3)

(3) *Stone pushed forward and then kicked back by the wheel. A small step down. The downward bump of the car swelled out the tyre momentarily.*

TRACK OF (1) AND (2) BICYCLE AND (3) MOTOR

damp earth that it may kick up from under the surface will dry very rapidly to the same colour as the surface dust, and the sharp edges of the footmarks will soon be rounded off by the breeze playing over the dry dust in which they are formed. When it gets into damp ground, the same track will look much fresher, because the sun will have only partially dried up the upturned soil, and the wind will not, therefore, have bevelled off the sharp edges of the impression, and if it gets into damp clay, under shade of trees, etc., where the sun does not get at it, the same track, which may have looked a day old in the sand, will here look quite fresh.

Of course, a great clue to the age of tracks will often be found in spots of rain having fallen on them since they were made (if

Horses' Tracks

Walking.

Trotting.

Canter.

O.F.   O.H.   N.H.   N.F.   O.F.

6'-6"   3'-10"   7'-6"   5'-0"

O.H.= Off Hind, etc.

Galloping.

Lame Horse Walking: Which leg is he lame in?
N.B.—The long feet are the hind feet.

These are the tracks of two birds on the ground. One lives
generally on the ground, the other in bushes and trees. Which
track belongs to which bird?

you know at what time the rain fell), dust or grass seeds blown
into them (if you noticed at what time the wind was blowing), or
the crossing of other tracks over the original ones, or where the
grass has been trodden down, the extent to which it has since dried
or withered. In following a horse, the length of time since it passed
can also be judged by the freshness, or otherwise, of the drop-
pings, due allowance being made for the effect of sun, rain or
birds, etc., upon them.

Having learned to distinguish the pace and age of spoor, you
must next learn to follow it over all kinds of ground. This is an
accomplishment that you can practise all your life, and you will
still find yourself learning at the end of it—you will find yourself
continually improving.

Then there is a great deal to learn from the ashes of fires—
whether they are still warm or cold, scraps showing what kind of
food the people were eating, whether plentiful or scarce.

You must not only keep a sharp look-out for scout signs made
by your own Scouts, but also for those made by hostile Scouts.
Foreign Scouts also have their private signs—as also do tramps.
The following are some of the signs made by tramps on walls or
fences near houses where they have been begging, which they
chalk up to warn others of their class:

⊙   Very bad: they give you   ⋋   No good.
      in charge here.

△   Too many tramps have   ☐   Bad people.
      been here already.

Mr. Deakin, who was Premier of Australia, told me how he
travelled on board ship with a number of natives of Australia who
were on the sea for the first time in their lives.

When the ship got out to sea he noticed all these natives had
got into the bows and were lying flat on the deck with their heads
over the side staring intently into the water ahead of the ship. So
interested were they in the water that for some time he could not
get any reply to his question as to what they were looking at, till
at length one of them said: "We cannot understand how the ship
is finding its way across the sea; we cannot see the trail that it is
following; we know that our eyes are sharp enough on shore, and
often when we are guiding white men along a trail they say they
cannot see the tracks which to us are clear enough—their eyes are
different from ours. But here at sea the English sailors evidently
can see tracks ahead of them, otherwise they would not know

· which way to send the ship, and yet we, who are so good at seeing on shore, cannot see any sign of a track or mark on the water."

When getting on to very fresh spoor of man or beast, the old scout will generally avoid following it closely, because the hunted animal will frequently look back to see if it is being followed. The tracker therefore makes a circle, and comes back on to where he would expect to find the spoor again. If he finds it, he makes another circle farther ahead till he finds no spoor. Then he knows he is ahead of his game, so he gradually circles nearer and nearer till he finds it, taking care of course not to get to windward of the animal when within scenting distance.

Hints on Spooring

In tracking where the spoor is difficult to see, such as on hard ground, or in grass, note the direction of the last footprint that you can see, then look on in the same direction, but well ahead of you, say, 20 or 30 yards, and in grass you will generally see the blades bent or trodden, and on hard ground, possibly stones displaced or scratched, and so on; small signs which, seen in a line one behind the other, give a kind of track that otherwise would not be noticed. I once tracked a bicycle on a hard macadam road where it really made no impression at all, but by looking along the surface of the road for a long distance ahead of me, under the rising sun as it happened, the line it had taken was quite visible through the almost invisible coating of dew upon the ground. Standing on the track and looking upon it close to my feet I could not see the slightest sign of it. The great thing is to look for a difficult track *against* the sun, so that the slightest dent in the ground throws a shadow.

If you lose sight of the track you must make a "cast" to find it again. To do this put your handkerchief, staff or other mark at the last footmark that you noticed, then work round it in a wide circle, say, 30, 50 or 100 yards away from it as a centre—choosing the most favourable ground, soft ground if possible, to find signs of the outward track. If you are with a Patrol it is generally best for the Patrol to halt while one or perhaps two men make the cast. If everybody starts trying to find the spoor they very soon defeat their object by treading it out or confusing it with their own footmarks—too many cooks easily spoil the broth in such a case.

In making a cast use your common sense as to which direction the enemy has probably taken, and try it there. I remember an instance of tracking a boar which illustrates what I mean. The

boar had been running through some muddy inundated fields, and
was easy enough to follow until he turned off over some very
hard and stony ground, where after a little while not a sign of his
spoor was to be seen. A cast had accordingly to be made. The last

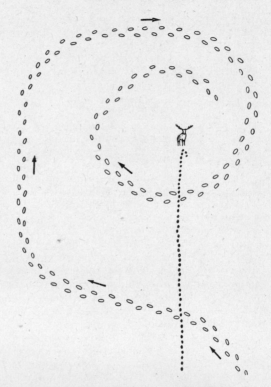

OLD HAND COMES ON A BUCK SPOOR

footmark was marked, and the tracker moved round a wide circle,
examining the ground most carefully, but not a sign was found.
Then the tracker took a look round the country, and, putting himself in place of the boar said, "Now which direction would I have
gone in?" Some distance to the front of him, as the original track
led, stood a long hedge of prickly cactus; in it were two gaps. The
tracker went to one of these as being the line the boar would

probably take. Here the ground was still very hard, and no foot-mark was visible, but on a leaf of the cactus in the gap was a pellet of wet mud; and this gave the desired clue; there was no mud on this hard ground, but the boar had evidently brought some on his feet from the wet ground he had been travelling through. This one little sign enabled the tracker to work on in the right direction to another and another, until eventually he got on to the spoor again in favourable ground, and was able to follow up the boar to his resting-place.

I have watched a tracker in the Sudan following tracks where for a time they were quite invisible to the ordinary eye in this way. While the track was clear he made his own stride exactly to fit that of the track, so that he walked step for step with it, and he tapped the ground with his staff as he walked along—ticking off each footprint as it were. When the footprints disappeared on hard ground, or had been buried by drifting sand, he still walked on at the same pace, tap-tapping the ground with his staff at the spot where there ought to have been a footprint. Occasionally he saw a slight depression or mark, which showed that there had been a footprint there, and thus he knew he was still on the right line.

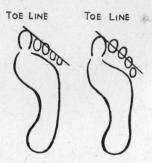

TOE LINE   TOE LINE

It is very puzzling for a beginner to tell the difference between a lot of footmarks of bare feet—they all look so much alike—but this is the way the Indian police trackers do it. It may come in useful some day for a Scout to know it in South Africa or Egypt, or other places where people go barefooted.

When measuring the footprint of the man you are after, draw a line from the tip of the big toe to the tip of the little toe, and then notice where the other toes come with regard to this line, and note it down in your pocket-book. Then when you come to a number of tracks you have only to try this same line on one or two of them till you find the one you want; all people vary a little in the position of their toes.

Try it with the other Scouts in your Patrol, each of you making a footprint with his bare foot, and then noting how it is different from the others when the toe line is drawn.

CAMP FIRE YARN. No. 13

READING "SIGN" OR DEDUCTION

WHEN a Scout has learned to notice "sign," he must then learn to "put this and that together," and so read a *meaning* from what he has seen. This is called "deduction." Here is an example of what I mean which was given in the *Forest and Stream* which shows how the young Scout can read the meaning from "sign" when he has been trained to it.

A cavalry soldier had got lost and some of his comrades were hunting all over the country to find him, when they came across a native boy, and asked him if he had seen the lost man. He immediately said: "Do you mean a very tall soldier, riding a roan horse that was slightly lame?"

They said, "Yes; that was the man. Where did you see him?"

The boy replied, "I have not seen him, but I know where he has gone."

Thereupon they arrested him, thinking that probably the man had been murdered and made away with, and that the boy had heard about it.

But eventually he explained that he had seen tracks of the man which he could point out to them.

Finally he brought them to a place where the signs showed that the man had made a halt. The horse had rubbed itself against a tree, and had left some of its hairs sticking to the bark, which showed that it was a roan horse; its hoof marks showed that it was lame, that is, one foot was not so deeply indented on the ground and did not take so long a pace as the other feet. That the rider was a soldier was shown by the imprint of his boot, which was an army boot. Then they asked the boy, "How could you tell that he was a tall man?" and the boy pointed out to where the soldier had broken a branch from the tree, which would have been out of reach of a man of ordinary height.

Deduction is exactly like reading a book.

A boy who has never been taught to read, and who sees you reading from a book, would ask, "How do you do it?" and you would point out to him that a number of small signs on a page are letters; these letters when grouped form words; and words form sentences; and sentences give information.

Similarly, a trained scout will see little signs and tracks, he puts them together in his mind, and quickly reads a meaning from them such as an untrained man would never arrive at.

And from frequent practice he gets to read the meaning at a glance, just as you do a book, without the delay of spelling out each word, letter by letter.

I was one day, during the Matabele War, with a native out scouting near to the Matoppo Hills over a wide grassy plain. Suddenly we crossed a track freshly made in grass, where the blades of grass were still green and damp, though pressed down; all were bending one way, which showed the direction in which the people had been travelling; following up the track for a bit it got on to a patch of sand, and we then saw that it was the spoor of several women (small feet with straight edge, and short steps) and boys (small feet, curved edge, and longer strides), walking, not running, towards the hills, about five miles away; where we believed the enemy to be hiding.

Then we saw a leaf lying about ten yards off the track. There were no trees for miles, but we knew that trees having this kind of leaf grew at a village fifteen miles away, in the direction from which the footmarks were coming. It seemed likely therefore that the women had come from that village, bringing the leaf with them, and had gone to the hills.

On picking up the leaf we found it was damp, and smelled of native beer. The short steps showed that the women were carrying loads. So we guessed that according to the custom they had been carrying pots of native beer on their heads, the mouths of the pots being stopped up with bunches of leaves. One of these leaves had fallen out; but we found it ten yards off the track, which showed that at the time it fell a wind was blowing. There was no wind now, i.e. seven o'clock, but there had been some about five o'clock.

So we guessed from all these little signs that a party of women and boys had brought beer during the night from the village 15 miles away, and had taken it to the enemy on the hills, arriving there soon after six o'clock.

The men would probably start to drink the beer at once (as it goes sour in a few hours), and would, by the time we could get there, be getting sleepy and keeping a bad look-out, so we should have a favourable chance of looking at their positions.

We accordingly followed the women's track, found the enemy, made our observations, and got away with our information without any difficulty.

And it was chiefly done on the evidence of that one leaf. So you see the importance of noticing even a little thing like that.

Instances of Deduction

By noticing very small signs detectives have discovered crimes.

In one case a crime had been committed, and a stranger's coat was found which gave no clue to the owner. The coat was put into a stout bag, and beaten with a stick. The dust was collected from the bag and examined under a powerful magnifying-glass, and was found to consist of fine sawdust, which showed that the owner of the coat was probably a carpenter, or sawyer, or joiner. The dust was then put under a more powerful magnifying-glass—called a microscope—and it was then seen that it also contained some tiny grains of gelatine and powdered glue. These things are not used by carpenters or sawyers, so the coat was shown to belong to a joiner, and the police got on to the track of the criminal.

Dust out of pockets, or in the recesses of a pocket-knife, and so on, if closely examined, tells a great deal.

Dr. Bell, of Edinburgh, is said to be the original from whom Sir Arthur Conan Doyle drew his idea of Sherlock Holmes.

The doctor was once teaching a class of medical students at a hospital how to doctor people. A patient was brought in, so that the doctor might show how an injured man should be treated. The patient in this case came limping in, and the doctor turned to one of the students and asked him:

"What is the matter with this man?"

The student replied, "I don't know, sir. I haven't asked him."

The doctor said: "Well, there is no need to ask him, you should see for yourself—he has injured his right knee; he is limping on that leg; he injured it by burning it in the fire; you see how his trouser is burnt away at the knee. This is Monday morning. Yesterday was fine; Saturday was wet and muddy. The man's trousers are muddy all over. He had a fall in the mud on Saturday night."

Then he turned to the man and said: "You drew your wages on Saturday and got drunk, and in trying to get your clothes dry by the fire when you got home, you fell on the fire and burnt your knee—isn't that so?"

"Yes, sir," replied the man.

True Scouting Stories

Captain Stigand in *Scouting and Reconnaissance in Savage Countries,* gives the following instances of scouts reading important meaning from small signs.

When he was going round outside his camp one morning, he noticed fresh spoor of a horse which had been walking. He knew that all his horses only went at a jog-trot, so it must have been a stranger's horse.

So he recognised that a mounted scout of the enemy had been quietly looking at his camp in the night.

Coming to a village in Central Africa from which the inhabitants had fled, he could not tell what tribe it belonged to till he found a crocodile's foot in one of the huts, which showed that the village belonged to the Awisa tribe, as they eat crocodiles, and the neighbouring tribes do not.

A man was seen riding a camel over half a mile away. A native who was watching him said, "It is a man of slave blood." "How can you tell at this distance?" "Because he is swinging his leg. A true Arab rides with his legs close to the camel's side."

General Joubert, who was Commander-in-Chief of the Boer Army in the Boer War, 1900, told me (some years before that) that in the previous Boer War, 1881, it was his wife who first noticed the British troops were occupying Majuba Mountain. The Boers were at that time camped near the foot of the mountain, and they generally had a small party of men on the top as a lookout. On this particular day they had intended moving away early in the morning, so the usual picket had not been sent up on to the mountain.

While they were getting ready to start, Mrs. Joubert, who evidently had the eyes of a scout, looked up and said, "Why, there is an Englishman on the top of Majuba!" The Boers said, "No—it must be our own men who have gone up there, after all." But Mrs. Joubert stuck to it, and said, "Look at the way he walks, that is no Boer—it is an Englishman." And so it was; she was right. An English force had climbed the mountain during the night, but by the stupidity of this man showing himself up on the sky-line, their presence was immediately detected by the Boers, who, instead of being surprised by them, climbed up the mountain unseen under the steep crags, and surprised the British, and drove them off with heavy loss.

An officer lost his field-glasses during some manœuvres on the desert five miles from Cairo, and he sent for the native trackers to look for them.

They came and asked to see the tracks of his horse; the horse was brought out and led about, so that they could see his footprints. These they carried in their minds, and went out to where the manœuvres had been: there, among the hundreds of hoof marks of the cavalry and artillery, they very soon found those of the officer's horse, and followed them up wherever he had ridden, till they found the field-glasses lying where they had dropped out of their case on the desert.

These trackers are particularly good at spooring camels. To anyone not accustomed to them, the footmark of one camel looks very like that of any other camel, but to a trained eye they are all as different as people's faces, and these trackers remember them very much as you would remember the faces of people you had seen.

Some years ago a camel was stolen near Cairo. The police tracker was sent for and shown its spoor. He followed it for a long way until it got into some streets, where it was entirely lost among other footmarks. But a year later this police tracker suddenly came on the fresh track of this camel; he had remembered its appearance all that time. It had evidently been walking with another camel whose footmark he knew was that of one which belonged to a well-known camel thief. So, without trying to follow the tracks when they got into the city, he went with a policeman straight to the man's stable, and there found the long-missing camel.

The "Gauchos," or native cowboys, of South America are fine scouts. Though the cattle lands are now for the most part enclosed, they used formerly to have to track stolen and lost beasts for miles, and were therefore very good trackers. The story is told that one of these men was sent to track a stolen horse, but failed to follow it up. Ten months later, when in a different part of the country, he suddenly noticed the fresh spoor of this horse on the ground. He had remembered its appearance all that time. He at once followed it up and recovered it for his master.

Example of Practice in Deduction

A simple deduction from signs noticed in my walk one morning on a stormy mountain path in Kashmir.

Sign Observed.—Tree-stump, about 3 feet high, by the path. A stone about the size of a coco-nut lying near it, to which were sticking some bits of bruised walnut rind, dried up. Some walnut rind also lying on the stump. Farther along the path, 30 yards to the south of the stump, were lying bits of walnut shell of four walnuts. Close by was a high sloping rock, alongside the path. The only walnut tree in sight was 150 yards north of the stump.

At the foot of the stump was a cake of hardened mud which showed the impression of a grass shoe.

What would you make out from those signs? My solution of it was this:

A man had gone southward on a long journey along the path two days ago carrying a load; and had rested at the rock while he ate walnuts.

My deductions were these:

It was a man carrying a load, because carriers when they want to rest do not sit down, but rest their load against a sloping rock and lean back. Had he had no load, he would probably have sat down on the stump, but he preferred to go 30 yards farther to where the rock was. Women do not carry loads there, so it was a man. But he first broke the shells of his walnuts on the tree-stump with the stone, having brought them from the tree 150 yards north. So he was travelling south, and he was on a long journey, as he was wearing shoes, and not going barefooted, as he would be if only strolling near his home. Three days ago there was rain, the cake of mud had been picked up while the ground was still wet—but it had not been since rained upon, and was now dry. The walnut rind was also dry, and confirmed the time that had elapsed.

There is no important story attached to this, but it is just an example of everyday practice which should be carried out by Scouts.

CAMP FIRE YARN.   No. 14

STALKING

A<small>T</small> some manœuvres two hostile patrols of soldiers were approaching, looking for each other, till the ground between them became very open, and it seemed hopeless for a scout to cross it without being seen. However, a small ditch of about two feet deep and overgrown with bushes ran across part of the open plain from the point where one patrol was lying hidden. They noticed two calves which came out on to the plain from the opposite side, and walked across the open till they got to the end of this ditch, and here they stopped and separated and began browsing.

A scout now started to make use of this ditch by crawling along it till he should get to the far end near the calves, and there he hoped to find some way of getting on farther, or of at least peeping out and getting a nearer view of the possible position of the enemy. When about half-way along the ditch, he was suddenly fired at by an enemy's scout already there, in the ditch.

When the umpire rode up and asked him how he had got there without being seen, the hostile scout said that finding he could not reach the ditch without being seen if he went across the plain, he seized two calves which he had found among the bushes where his patrol were hiding, and, stepping between them, he drove the pair of them, by holding their tails, across to the open ditch; here he let them go, and slid himself into the ditch without being noticed.

How to Hide Yourself

When you want to observe wild animals you have to stalk them, that is, to creep up to them without their seeing or smelling you.

A hunter when he is stalking wild animals keeps himself entirely hidden, so does the war scout when watching or looking for the enemy; a policeman does not catch pickpockets by standing about in uniform watching for them; he dresses like one of the crowd, and as often as not gazes into a shop window and sees all that goes on behind him reflected as if in a looking-glass.

If a guilty person finds himself being watched, it puts him on his guard, while an innocent person becomes annoyed. So, when you are observing a person, don't do so by openly staring at them, but notice the details you want to at one glance or two, and if you want to study them more, walk behind them; you can learn just as much from a back view, in fact more than you can from a front view, and, unless they are Scouts and look round frequently, they do not know that you are observing them.

War scouts and hunters stalking game always carry out two important rules when they don't want to be seen.

One is—they take care that the ground behind them, or trees or buildings, etc., are of the same colour as their clothes.

And the other is—if an enemy or a deer is seen looking for them they remain perfectly still without moving so long as he is there.

FIND THE MAN HIDDEN IN THE OPEN

In that way a Scout, even though he is out in the open, will often escape being noticed.

In choosing your background, consider the colour of your clothes; thus, if you are dressed in khaki, don't go and stand in front of a white-washed wall, or in front of a dark-shaded bush, but go where there is khaki-coloured sand or grass or rocks behind you —and remain perfectly still. It will be very difficult for an enemy to distinguish you, even at a short distance.

If you are in dark clothes, get among dark bushes, or in the shadow of trees or rocks, but be careful that the ground beyond you is also dark—if there is light-coloured ground beyond the trees under which you are standing, for instance, you will stand out clearly defined against it.

If you are in red, try and get against red-brick buildings, or red earth or rocks, and so on.

In making use of hills as look-out places, be very careful not to show yourself on the top or sky-line. That is the fault which a tenderfoot generally makes.

It is quite a lesson to watch a Zulu scout making use of a hill-top on rising ground as a look-out place. He will crawl up on all fours, lying flat in the grass; on reaching the top he will very slowly raise his head, inch by inch, till he can see the view. If he sees the enemy on beyond, he will have a good look, and if he thinks they are watching him, will keep his head perfectly steady for an immense time, hoping that he will be mistaken for a stump or a stone. If he is not detected, he will very gradually lower his head, inch by inch, into the grass again, and crawl quietly away. Any quick or sudden movement of the head on the sky-line would be very liable to attract attention, even at a considerable distance.

At night, keep as much as possible in low ground, ditches, etc., so that you are down in the dark, while an enemy who does come near will be visible to you outlined on higher ground against the stars.

By squatting low in the shadow of the bush at night, and keeping quite still, I have let an enemy's scout come and stand within three feet of me, so that when he turned his back towards me I was able to stand up where I was, and fling my arms round him.

A point also to remember in keeping hidden while moving, especially at night, is to walk quietly; the thump of an ordinary man's heel on the ground can be heard a good distance off, but a scout or hunter always walks lightly, on the ball of his feet, not on his heels; and this you should practise whenever you are walking, by day or by night, indoors as well as out, so that it becomes a habit with you—so as to walk as lightly and silently as possible. You will find that as you grow into it your power of walking long distances will grow, you will not tire so soon as you would if clumping along in the heavy-footed manner of most people.

Remember always that to stalk a wild animal, or a good scout, you must keep down wind of him, even if the wind is so slight as to be merely a faint air.

Before starting to stalk your enemy, then, you should be sure which way the wind is blowing, and work up against it. To find this out, you should wet your thumb all round with your tongue, then hold it up and see which side feels coldest, or you can throw some light dust, or dry grass or leaves in the air, and see which way they drift.

The Red Indian scouts, when they wanted to reconnoitre an enemy's camp, used to tie a wolf's skin on their backs and walk on all fours, and, imitating the howl of a wolf, prowl round the camps at night.

In Australia, the natives stalk emus—which are great birds something like an ostrich—by putting an emu's skin over themselves, and walking with body bent and one hand held up to represent the bird's head and neck.

American scouts, when peeping over a ridge or any place where

SCOUT STALKING SCOUT

This sketch is of an incident which happened during the siege of
Mafeking. I had crept out in the early morning to reconnoitre the
position of the enemy's big gun, and while lying hidden amongst
some rocks, I saw a man with a black face cautiously stalking towards the town. Presuming him to be an enemy, I laid low until
he came close, and I then saw that he was a white man in disguise,
and recognised him as one of my own men returning from scouting the enemy.

their head might be seen against the sky-line, put on a cap made
of wolf's-head skin with ears on it—so that they may be mistaken
for a wolf, if seen.

Our scouts also, when looking out among grass, etc., tie a string
or band round their head, and stick a lot of grass in it, some upright, some drooping over their face, so that their head is invisible.

When hiding behind a big stone or mound, etc., they don't look
over the top, but round the side of it.

CAMP FIRE YARN. No. 15

ANIMALS

Scouts in many parts of the world use the calls of wild animals and birds for communicating with each other, especially at night or in thick bush, or in fog, etc., but it is also very useful to be able to imitate the calls if you want to watch the habits of the animals. You can begin by calling chickens; or by talking to dogs in dog language, and you very soon find you can give the angry growl or the playful growl of a dog. Owls, wood-pigeons and curlews are very easily called.

Mr. William Long in his very interesting book, called *Beasts of the Field,* describes how he once called a moose. The moose is a very huge kind of stag, with an ugly, bulging kind of nose. He lives in the forests of North America and Canada, and is very hard to get near; and is pretty dangerous when he is angry.

Mr. Long was in a canoe, fishing, when he heard a bull-moose calling in the forest—so just for fun he went ashore and cut a strip of bark off a birch tree and rolled it up into a cone or trumpet shape so as to make a kind of megaphone (about fifteen inches long, five inches wide at the larger end, and about an inch or two at the mouth-piece). With this he proceeded to imitate the roaring grunt of the bull-moose. The effect was tremendous; the old moose came tearing down and even came into the water and tried to get at him—and it was only by hard paddling that in the end he got away.

One of the best things in scouting is the hunting of big game— that is, going after elephants, lions, rhino, wild boar, deer and those kinds of animals; and a fellow has to be a pretty good scout if he hopes to succeed at it.

You get plenty of excitement and plenty of danger, too; and all that I have told you about observation and tracking and hiding yourself comes in here. And, in addition to these, you must know all about animals and their habits and ways if you want to be successful.

I have said the "hunting" or "going after" big game is one of the best things in scouting. I did not say shooting or killing the game was the best part; for, as you get to study animals, you get to like them more and more, and you will soon find that you don't want to kill them for the mere sake of killing, and that the more you see of them the more you see the wonderful work of God in them.

All the fun of hunting lies in the adventurous life in the jungle, the chance in many cases of the animal hunting *you* instead of you hunting the animal, the interest of tracking him up, stalking him and watching all that he does and learning his habits. The actual shooting the animal that follows is only a very small part of the fun.

No Scout should ever kill an animal unless there is some real reason for doing so, and in that case he should kill it quickly and effectively, so as to give it as little pain as possible.

In fact, many big-game hunters nowadays prefer to shoot their game with the camera instead of with the rifle—which gives just as interesting results—except when you and your natives are hungry, then you must, of course, kill your game.

My brother was once big-game shooting in East Africa and had very good sport with the camera, living in the wilds, and tracking and stalking and finally snapshotting elephants, rhinoceroses and other big animals.

One day he had crept up near to an elephant and had set up his camera and had got his head under the cloth, focusing it, when

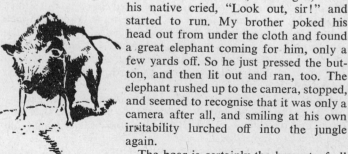

his native cried, "Look out, sir!" and started to run. My brother poked his head out from under the cloth and found a great elephant coming for him, only a few yards off. So he just pressed the button, and then lit out and ran, too. The elephant rushed up to the camera, stopped, and seemed to recognise that it was only a camera after all, and smiling at his own irritability lurched off into the jungle again.

The boar is certainly the bravest of all

animals; he is the real "King of the Jungle," and the other animals all know it. If you watch a drinking pool in the jungle at night, you will see the animals that come to it all creeping down nervously, looking out in every direction for hidden enemies. But when the boar comes he simply swaggers down with his great head and its shiny tusks swinging from side to side; he cares for nobody, but everybody cares for him; even a tiger drinking at the pool will give a snarl and sneak quickly out of sight.

I have often lain out on moonlight nights to watch the animals, especially wild boars, in the jungle; and it is just as good fun as merely going after them to kill them.

And I have caught and kept a young wild boar and a young panther, and found them most amusing and interesting little beggars. The boar used to live in my garden, and he never became really tame, though I got him as a baby.

He would come to me when I called him—but very warily; he would never come to a stranger, and a native he would "go for" and try and cut him with his little tusks.

He used to practise the use of his tusks while turning at full speed round an old tree stump in the garden, and he would gallop at this and round it in a figure of eight continuously for over five minutes at a time, and then fling himself down on his side panting with his exertions.

Of course a Scout who lives in the country has much better chances of studying animals and birds than in a town.

Still, if you live in London there are lots of different kinds of birds in the parks, ducks and waterfowl of every kind, pelicans, woodpigeons, woodpeckers and most of the English birds; there is almost every animal under the sun to be seen alive in the Zoological Gardens, or stuffed and set up in the Natural History Museum at South Kensington—so that a Boy Scout in London ought to know as much about all animals as most people. And even in Leadenhall Market you can see a number of different kinds of live animals for sale, as well as in the many animal shops about London or any other big town.

In other towns it is perhaps a little more difficult, but most of them have their Natural History Museum, where a fellow can learn the appearance and names of many animals; and you can do a lot of observing in the parks or by starting a feeding-box for birds at your own window. And, best of all, by going out into the country whenever you get a few hours for it by train, or bicycle, or on your own flat feet, and there stalk such animals as rabbits, hares, water-rats, birds, fish, etc., and watch all they do, and get to know the different kinds and their names, and also what kind of tracks they make on the ground, their nests and eggs, and so on.

If you are lucky enough to own a camera, you cannot possibly do better than start making a collection of photos of animals and birds taken from life. Such a collection is ten times more interesting than the ordinary boy's collection of stamps, or crests, or autographs, which any ass can accomplish by sitting at home and bothering other people to give.

The wild animals I shall talk of now are those which you find in Great Britain. Any Scouts who live in our overseas Dominions or elsewhere must make up their own lists for themselves.

As a Scout you should study the habits of as many of these animals as you can:

Red Deer	Badgers	Otters	Hedgehogs
Hares	Foxes	Fallow Deer	Voles
Rabbits	Weasels	Bats	Squirrels
Rats	Stoats	Moles	Polecats
Mice			

Birds

A man who studies birds is called an ornithologist. Mark Twain, the amusing yet kind-hearted American writer, says: "There are fellows who write books about birds and love them so much that they'll go hungry and tired to find a new kind of bird —and kill it.

"They are called 'ornithologers.'

"I could have been an 'ornithologer' myself, because I always loved birds and creatures. And I started out to learn how to be one. I saw a bird sitting on a dead limb of a high tree, singing away with his head tilted back and his mouth open—and before I thought I fired my gun at him; his song stopped all suddenly, and he fell from the branch, limp like a rag, and I ran and picked him up—and he was dead: his body was warm in my hand, and his head rolled about this way and that, like as if his neck was broke, and there was a white skin over his eyes, and one drop of red blood sparkled on the side of his head—and—laws! I couldn't see nothing for the tears. I haven't ever murdered no creature since then that warn't doing me no harm—and I ain't agoing to neither."

A good Scout is generally a good "ornithologer," as Mark Twain calls him. That is to say, he likes stalking birds and watching all that they do. He discovers, by watching them, where and how they build their nests.

He does not, like the ordinary boy, want to go and rob them of their eggs, but he likes to watch how they hatch out their young and teach them to feed themselves and to fly. He gets to know every species of bird by its call and by its way of flying; and he knows which birds remain all the year round and which only come at certain seasons; and what kind of food they like best, and how they change their plumage; what sort of nests they build, where they build them, and what the eggs are like.

There are 177 different kinds of birds in Great Britain. Here are some of the commoner birds which a Scout should know by sight and sound:

Woodpigeon	Wild goose	Gull	Raven
Pheasant	Robin	Tern	Thrush
Partridge	Starling	Owl	Blackbird
Grouse (Scotland)	Heron	Hawk	Tit
Cuckoo	Wren	Falcon	Finch
Skylark	Wagtail	Moorhen	Woodcock
Snipe	Swallow	Jackdaw	Curlew
Wild duck	Martin	Rook	Kingfisher
Plover	Woodpecker	Crow	

A good deal of natural history can even be studied by keeping birds in your houses, or watching them in your neighbourhood, especially if you feed them daily in winter. It is interesting to note, for instance, their different ways of singing, how some sing to make love to the hen birds, while others, like the barndoor cock, crow or sing to challenge another to fight. A herring gull makes an awful ass of himself when he tries to sing and to show himself off to the ladies, and an old crow is not much better. Then it is interesting to watch how the young birds hatch out: some appear naked, with no feathers, and their eyes shut and their mouths open. Others, with fluffy kind of feathers all over them, are full of life and energy. Young moorhens, for instance, swim as soon as they come out of the egg; young chickens start running about and hunting flies within a very few minutes; while a young sparrow is useless for days, and has to be fed and coddled by his parents.

CA-CAW

There are over forty different kinds of birds which visit England from abroad, especially from India and Africa, at certain times of the year, chiefly in April, such as the sand martin, swallow, house martin, nightingale, hobby falcon, cuckoo, corncrake, and swift.

A good many birds are almost dying out in Great Britain because so many boys bag all their eggs when they find their nests.

Birds'-nesting is very like big-game shooting—you look out in places that, as a hunter, you know are likely places for the birds you want; you watch the birds fly in and out and you find the nest. But do not then go and destroy the nest and take all the eggs. If you are actually a collector, take one egg and leave the rest, and, above all, don't pull the nest about, otherwise the parent birds will desert it, and all those eggs, which might have developed into jolly young birds, will be wasted.

Far better than taking the eggs is to take a photo, or make a sketch of the hen sitting on her nest, or to make a collection of pictures of the different kinds of nests made by the different kinds of birds.

Through ignorance of natural history, many keepers and others see no difference between sparrow-hawks, merlins, and kestrels, and destroy all of them as mischievous to game. Sparrow-hawks and merlins do, no doubt, kill young game, but a kestrel hardly ever, if ever. He lives principally on field mice. You can tell him by his flight—he spends much of his time hovering in the air, looking out with his sharp eyes for a mouse upon which to swoop down. The sparrow-hawk flits in and out round rocks and over fences, hoping thus to come on prey by surprise. The merlin is a very small but very plucky little hawk, and hunts down his prey by fast flying.

Reptiles and Fishes

The more usual reptiles in Great Britain are:—

Grass Snake   Viper   Lizard

The commoner fishes are:—

Trout	Dace	Pike
Grayling	Chub	Minnow
Perch	Bream	Salmon
Roach		

and a number of sea fish.

Every Scout ought to be able to fish in order to get food for himself. A tenderfoot who starved on the bank of a river full of fish would look very silly, yet it might happen to one who had never learned to catch fish.

And fishing brings out a lot of the points in Scouting, especially if you fish with a fly. To be successful you must know a lot about the habits and ways of the fish, what kind of haunt he frequents, in what kind of weather he feeds and at what time of day, which kind of food he likes best, how far off he can see you, and so on. Without knowing these, you can fish away until you are blue in the face and never catch one.

A fish generally has his own particular haunt in the stream, and when once you discover a fish at home you can go and creep near and watch all that he does.

Then you have to be able to tie very special knots with delicate gut, which is a bit of a puzzler to any boy whose fingers are all thumbs.

I will only give you one or two here, but there are many others. These are drawn half tied, just before pulling tight.

Here is the overhandloop: To join a line to a loop do it this way:

Much the same kind of knot is used to tie a hook to a line:

To join two lengths of line together, even when of different thickness, follow out this method:

And you have to have infinite patience; your line gets caught up in bushes and reeds, or your clothes—or when it can't find any other body it ties up in a knot round itself. Well, it's no use getting angry with it. There are only two things to do—the first is to smile a smile and the second is to set to work very leisurely to undo it. Then you will have loads of disappointments in losing fish through the line breaking, or other mishaps: but remember those are what happen to everybody when they begin fishing, and are the troubles that in the end make it so very enjoyable when you have got over them.

And when you catch your fish do as I do—only keep those you specially want for food or as specimens; put back the others the moment you have landed them. The prick of the hook in their leathery mouth does not hurt them for long, and they swim off quite happily to enjoy life in their water again.

If you use a dry fly, that is, keeping your fly sitting on top of the water instead of sunk under the surface, you have really to stalk your fish, just as you would deer or any other game, for a trout is very sharp-eyed and shy.

You can also catch fish by netting, or, as scouts often have to do, by spearing them with a very sharp three-pronged spear. I have done it many a time, but it requires practice to be successful.

As far as snakes go there are not, fortunately, many poisonous ones in England—only the viper is poisonous. It is differently marked from other snakes, having a black V or arrow-head mark on its head and a dark zig-zag line along its back. It is generally dark brown in colour. The viper is sometimes called adder.

A Viper (or Adder) has this marking on his head and neck; other snakes have none—in Great Britain.

Of course a Scout ought to know about snakes, because in almost all wild countries you come across plenty of them and many of them dangerous.

They have a horrid knack of creeping into tents and under blankets, or into boots. You will always notice an old hand in camp before he turns in at night look very carefully through his blankets, and in the morning before putting on his boots he will carefully shake them out. I even find myself doing it now at home, just from habit.

Snakes don't like crawling over anything rough as a rule; so in India you often construct a kind of path, made of sharp, jagged stones, all round a house to prevent snakes crawling into it from the garden.

And on the prairie, hunters lay a hair rope on the ground in a circle round their blankets.

A hair rope has so many tiny spikes sticking out of it that it tickles the snake's tummy to such an extent he cannot go over it.

I used to catch snakes when I was at school by using a long stick with a small fork at the end of it. When I saw a snake I stalked him, jammed the fork down on his neck, and then tied him up the stick with strips of old handkerchief, and carried him back to sell to anybody who wanted a pet. But they are not good things to make pets of as a rule, because so many people have a horror of them, and it is not fair, therefore, to have them about in a house where servants or others might get frightened by them.

Poisonous snakes carry their poison in a small kind of bag inside their mouths. They have two fangs or long pointed teeth, which are on a kind of hinge; they lie flat along the snake's gums till he gets angry and wants to kill something; then they stand on end, and he dives his head forward and strikes them into his enemy. As he does so, the poison passes out of the poisonbag, or gland as it is called, into the two holes in the skin made by the fangs. This poison then gets into the veins of the man who has been bitten and is carried by the blood all over the body in a few seconds, unless steps are at once taken to stop it by sucking the wound and binding the veins up very tightly. It does no harm when swallowed.

Insects

Insects are very interesting animals to collect, or to watch, or to photograph.

Also for a Scout who fishes, or studies birds or reptiles, it is most important that he should know a certain amount about the insects which are their favourite food at different times of the year or different hours of the day.

The usual insects about which a Scout ought to know something are : —

Moths	Gnats	Bees and Wasps
Grasshoppers	Ants	Beetles
Glow-worms	Butterflies	Lice

About bees alone, whole books have been written—for they have wonderful powers in making their honeycomb, in finding their way for miles—sometimes as far as six miles—to find the right kind of flowers for giving them the sugary juice for making honey, and getting back with it to the hive.

They are quite a model community, for they respect their queen and kill those who won't work.

Then some insects are useful as food. Ants make a substitute for salt. Locusts—a big kind of grasshopper—are eaten in India and South Africa. We were very glad to get a flight or two of them over Mafeking. When they settled on the ground we went, and, with empty sacks, beat them down as they turned to rise. They were then dried in the sun and pounded up and eaten.

It doesn't sound very exciting to watch insects, but the great French naturalist, Henri Fabre, the son of peasants, spent days in studying the lives and habits of insects, and found out all kinds of curious things about them.

Some insects are our friends—like the silkworm and the lady-bird—but others are our enemies: thus, there are garden pests, like the green flies on rose trees and the turnip fly which attacks that vegetable. You all know how the mosquito spreads such dangerous diseases as malaria and yellow fever; and I need not remind you of how the house-fly can carry disease germs—that is why in camp, as well as at home, all food should be kept carefully covered, and no dirt or rubbish be allowed to lie about.

The insect world is a wonderful world and full of romance. But it is a very varied world, for there are nearly 12,000 different kinds of insects in Great Britain alone!

TREES

VERY often a Scout has to describe country which he has seen, and if he says it is "well wooded," it would often be of great importance that the reader of his report should know what kind of trees the woods were composed of.

For instance, if the wood were of fir or larch trees it would mean you could get poles for building bridges; if it were palm trees, you know you could get coco-nuts (or dates if they were date palms), and the palm juice for drinking. Willow trees mean water close by.

Or if pine woods or sugar bush or gum trees it would mean lots of good fuel. And he must know a poplar tree by sight, so as not to use poplar wood in camp if there are any old scouts present—they have a superstition that poplar brings bad luck.

A Scout should therefore make a point of learning the names and appearances of the trees in his country.

He should get hold of a leaf of each kind and compare it with the leaf on the tree; and then get to know the general shape and appearance of each kind of tree, so as to be able to recognise it at a distance—and not only in summer, but also in winter.

Horse chestnut is not so called because horses like the chestnuts, but because it has on the bark of its smaller branches small marks like horse-shoes, with all the nails in them.

The common trees in Great Britain which a Scout should know by sight are:—

Oak	Poplar	Holly	Beech
Elm	Pine	Horse	Birch
Plane	Sycamore	Chestnut	Spanish
Cedar	Larch	Ash	Chestnut
Fir	Willow	Lime	Walnut

A Scout never damages a tree by hacking at it with his knife or axe. It does not take long to fell a tree, but it takes many years to grow one, so a Scout only cuts down a tree for a good reason, not just for the sake of using his axe. For every tree felled, two should be planted.

It is seldom necessary to chop trees even for firewood, as usually there is plenty of dead wood (which burns more easily) lying about on the ground; a dead branch can be broken off. But dead wood in a hedge should never be removed, as it has probably been put there by the farmer to fill a gap and so stop his sheep and cattle from straying.

A Scout is also very careful about fires; when he uses one he sees that it is well out before he leaves the place; the fire should be doused with water and earth, well stamped down and then the original turf—which was put on one side before making the fire —is put back so that hardly a trace is left.

The Canadians say, "One tree may make a million matches; one match may destroy a million trees."

How Woods Burn

Apple burns well with sweet smell.

Ash very good green or dry. Easy to chop and split. Lasts longer than others. Excellent mixed with soft woods.

Beech gives big flame, green or dry.

Birch lights easily, quickly and clearly.

Chestnut good only if seasoned.

Elder burns well, but with bitter smoke.

Elm bad to light. Only smoulders. Little flame.

Holly burns well green. Makes good embers.

Lime, if dry, gives good heat.

Maple, if dry, gives good heat.

Oak burns steadily and slowly.

Pines good for kindling, but burn quickly.

Sycamore must be dry, gives good heat.

CAMP FIRE YARN. No. 17

HOW TO GROW STRONG

A Scout's Endurance

A scout lay sick in hospital in India with that most fatal disease called cholera. The doctor told the native man in attendance on him that the only chance of saving his life was violently to warm up his feet and keep the blood moving in his body by constantly rubbing him. The moment the doctor's back was turned, the native gave up rubbing and squatted down to have a quiet smoke. The poor patient, though he could not speak, understood all that was going on, and he was so enraged at the conduct of the native attendant that he resolved then and there that he would get well if only to give the native a lesson. Having made up his mind to get well he *got* well.

A scout's motto is "Never say die till you're dead"—and if he acts up to this it will pull him out of many a bad place when everything seems to be going wrong for him. It means a mixture of pluck, patience and strength, which we call "endurance."

Exercises and Their Object

There is a great deal of nonsense done in the way of bodily exercises; so many people seem to think that their only object is to make huge muscle. But to make yourself strong and healthy it is necessary to begin with your inside and to get the blood into good order and the heart to work well; that is the secret of the whole thing, and exercises of the body do it for you. This is the way—

(a) MAKE THE HEART STRONG in order to pump the blood properly to every part of the body, and so to build up flesh, bone and muscle.

(b) MAKE THE LUNGS STRONG in order to provide the blood with fresh air.

(c) MAKE THE SKIN PERSPIRE to get rid of the dirt from the blood.

(d) MAKE THE STOMACH WORK to feed the blood.

(e) MAKE THE BOWELS ACTIVE to remove the remains of food and dirt from the body.

(f) WORK MUSCLES IN EACH PART OF THE BODY to make the blood circulate to that part, and so increase your strength.

125

The secret of keeping well and healthy is to keep your blood clean and active. These different exercises will do that if you will use them every day. Someone has said, "If you practise body exercises every morning you will never be ill; and if you also drink a pint of hot water every night you will never die."

The blood thrives on simple good food, plenty of exercise, plenty of fresh air, cleanliness of the body both *inside* and out, and proper rest of body and mind at intervals.

An Easy Way to Keep Healthy

It is possible for any boy, even though he may be small and weak, to make himself into a strong and healthy man if he takes the trouble to do a few body exercises every day. They only take about ten minutes, and do not require any kind of apparatus such as dumb-bells, parallel bars, and so on.

They should be practised every morning, the first thing on getting up, and every evening before going to bed. It is best to do them with little or no clothing on, and in the open air, or close to an open window. The value of this exercise is much increased if you think of the object of each move while you are doing it, and if you are very particular to breathe the air in through your nose and to breathe out through your mouth—since breathing in through the nose prevents you from swallowing down all sorts of little seeds of poison or bad health, which are always floating about in the air—especially in rooms from which the fresh air is shut out; such rooms are very poisonous. A great many people who are pale and seedy, are made so by living in rooms where the windows are seldom opened and the air is full of unwholesome gases or germs. Open your windows, especially at the top, every day to let the foul air out.

Here are some good exercises. It strengthens the toes and feet to do these exercises barefooted.

1. THE HEAD.—Rub the head, face, and neck firmly over several times with the palms and fingers of both hands. Thumb the muscles of the neck and throat.

Brush your hair, clean your teeth, wash out your mouth and nose, drink a cup of cold water, and then go on with the following exercises.

The movements should all be done as slowly as possible.

2. THE CHEST.—From upright position bend to the front, arms stretched downwards, with back of the hands together in front of the knees. Breathe out.

Raise the hands gradually over the head and lean back as far as possible, drawing a deep breath *through the nose* as you do so—that is, drinking God's air into your lungs and blood. Lower the arms gradually to the sides, breathing out the word "Thanks" (to God) through the mouth.

FIG. 1

The right way.   The wrong way.

In the pictures → means drawing in the breath through the nose
←o means breathing out through the mouth.

Lastly, bend forward again, breathing out the last bit of breath in you, and saying the number of times you have done it, in order to keep count.

Repeat this exercise twelve times.

Remember while carrying it out that the object of the exercise is to develop shoulders, chest, heart, and breathing apparatus inside you.

3. THE STOMACH.—Standing upright, send out both arms, fingers extended, straight to the front, then slowly swing round to the right from the hips without moving the feet, and point the right arm as far round behind you as you can, keeping both arms level with, or a little higher than, the shoulders. Then, after a pause, swing slowly round as far as you can to the left. Repeat this a dozen times.

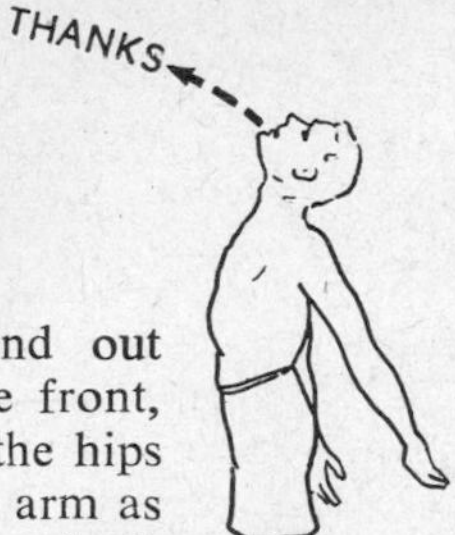

THANKS

FIG. 2.

This exercise is to move the inside organs such as liver and intestines, and help their work, as well as to strengthen the outside muscles round the ribs and stomach.

While carrying out this exercise, the breathing should be carefully regulated. Breathe in through the nose (not through the mouth), while pointing to the right rear; breathe out through the mouth as you come round and point to the left rear, and at the same time count aloud the number of the swing—or, what is better, thinking of it as part of your morning prayer with God, say aloud: "Bless Tim," "Bless Father," and any of your family or friends in turn.

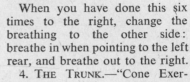

When you have done this six times to the right, change the breathing to the other side: breathe in when pointing to the left rear, and breathe out to the right.

4. THE TRUNK.—"Cone Exercise."—Standing at the "Alert," raise both hands as high as possible over the head, and link fingers, lean backwards, then sway the arms very slowly round in the direction of a cone, so that the hands make a wide circle above and around the body, the body turning from the hips, and leaning over to one side, then to the front, then to the other side, and then

BODY TWISTING

back; this is to exercise the muscles of the waist and stomach, and should be repeated, say, six times to either hand. With the eyes you should be trying to see all that goes on behind you during the movement.

A meaning attached to this exercise, which you should think of while carrying it out, is this: The clasping hands mean that you are knit together with friends—that is, other Scouts—all round you as you sway round to the right, left, before and behind you; in every direction you are bound to friends. Love

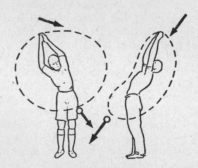

"CONE" EXERCISE

and friendship are the gift of God, so when you are making the upward move you look to Heaven and drink in the air and the good feeling, which you then breathe out to your comrades all round.

5. THE LOWER BODY.—Like every one of the exercises, this is, at the same time, a breathing exercise by which the lungs and heart are developed, and the blood made strong and healthy. You simply stand up and reach as high as you can skywards, and backwards, and then bend forward and downward till your fingers touch your toes *without bending your knees*.

Stand with the feet slightly apart, arms stretched overhead, hands together, and look up into the sky, leaning back as far as you can, as in Fig. 1.

If you mingle prayer with your exercises, as I described to you before, you can, while looking up in this way, say to God: "I am yours from top to toe," and drink in God's air (through your nose, not through the mouth). Then reach both hands upwards as far as possible (Fig. 2), breathe out the number of the turn

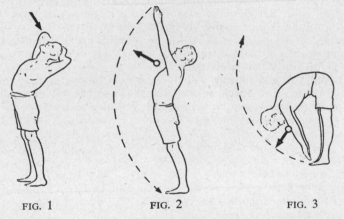

FIG. 1   FIG. 2   FIG. 3

that you are doing; then bend slowly forward and downward, knees stiff, till you touch your toes with your finger-tips (Fig. 3).

Tuck in the small of your back while on the downward bend.

Then, keeping arms and knees still stiff, gradually raise the body to the first position again, and repeat the exercise a dozen times.

The object of this exercise is, however, not to touch the toes, but to massage the stomach. If you find you cannot touch your toes do not force yourself to do it, and, more especially, do not jerk yourself or allow anyone else to force you down. The value of the exercise lies in the upward stroke as against the downward stroke.

6. THE LEGS AND TOES.—Standing, barefooted, at the position of "Alert." Put the hands on the hips, stand on tip-toe, turn the knees outwards, and bend them slowly till you gradually sink down to a squatting position, keeping the heels off the ground the whole time.

Then gradually raise the body and come to the first position again.

Repeat this a dozen times.

The small of the back must be tucked in. The breath should be drawn in through the nose, as the body rises, and counted out, through the mouth, as the body sinks. The weight of the body must be on the toes all the time, and the knees turned outwards to make your balance more easy. While performing the practice you should remember that its object is to strengthen the thighs, calves, and toe-sinews, as well as to exercise the stomach, so if you practise it more often in the day, at any odd moments, it will do you all the more good.

And you can connect with this exercise, since it makes you alternately stand up and squat down, that whether you are standing or sitting, at work or resting, you will hold yourself together (as your hands on your hips are doing), and make yourself do what is right.

These exercises are not merely intended as a way of passing time, but really to help a fellow to grow big as well as to grow strong.

Climbing.—Every boy likes climbing, and if you stick to it and become really good at it, you will go on at it for ever.

Most of the great mountain-climbers began as boys climbing up ropes and poles, and then trees. After that, a long way after—because if you haven't had lots of practice and strengthened your muscles you probably would tumble, and attend a funeral as the chief performer—you take up rock climbing, and so on to mountain climbing.

It is glorious sport teeming with adventure, but it needs strength in all your limbs, pluck, determination and endurance. But these all come with practice.

It is most important for mountain climbing to be able to keep your balance and to place your feet nimbly and quickly where you want them. For this there is nothing like the game of "Walking the Plank" along a plank set up on edge, "stepping stones" laid about on the ground at varying distances and angles to each other, and "Morris Dancing."

When I was a fairly active young bounder I went in for skirt-dancing. It amused people at our regimental theatricals and it was good exercise for me. But I came to realise a new value in it later on when I had to carry out some scouting on service against the Matabele in South Africa.

I had climbed into their mountain fastnesses in the Matoppo Hills and was discovered by them. I had to run for it. Their

great aim was to catch me alive as they wanted to give me something more special in the execution line than a mere shot through the head; they had some form of unpleasant torture in view for me. So when I ran I ran heartily.

The mountain consisted largely of huge granite boulders piled one on another. My running consisted largely in leaping down

from one boulder to another, and then it was that the balance
and foot management gained in skirt-dancing came to my aid. As
I skipped down the mountain I found myself out-distancing my
pursuers with the greatest of ease. These, being plainsmen, did
not understand rock-trotting and were laboriously slithering and
clambering down the boulders after me. So I got away; and with
the confidence thus engendered I paid many successful visits to
the mountains after this.

CAMP FIRE YARN. No. 18

HEALTH-GIVING HABITS

How to Keep Healthy

A LL the great peace scouts who have succeeded in exploring or hunting expeditions in wild countries have only been able to get on by being pretty good doctors themselves; because diseases, accidents and wounds are always being suffered by them or their men, and they don't find doctors and chemists' shops in the jungles to cure them. So that a Scout who does not know something about doctoring would never get on at all; he might just as well stay at home for all the good he will be.

Therefore practise keeping healthy yourself, and then you will be able to show others how to keep themselves healthy, too.

Keep Yourself Clean

If you cut your hand when it is dirty it is very likely to fester, and to become very sore; but if your hand is quite clean and freshly washed, no harm will come of it; it heals up at once.

Cleaning your skin helps to clean your blood. Doctors say that half the good of exercise is lost if you do not have a bath immediately after it.

It may not be always possible for you to get a bath every day, but you can, at any rate, rub yourself over with a wet towel, or scrub yourself with a dry one, and you ought not to miss a single day in doing this if you want to keep fit and well.

You should also keep clean in your clothing, both your underclothing as well as that which shows. Beat it out with a stick every day before putting it on.

And to be healthy and strong, you *must* keep your blood healthy and clean inside you. This is done by breathing in lots of pure, fresh air, by deep breathing, and by clearing out all dirty matter from inside your stomach, which is done by having a "rear" daily, without fail; many people are the better for having it twice a day. If there is any difficulty about it one day, drink plenty of good water, especially before and just after breakfast, and practise body-twisting exercises, and all should be well.

Never start work in the morning without some sort of food inside you, if it is only a cup of hot water. There is no need to take all the drugs, pills and medicines which you see so temptingly advertised; they often do you harm in the end. Never bathe in deep water very soon after a meal, it is very likely to cause cramp, which doubles you up, and so you get drowned.

Smoking

A scout does not smoke. Any boy can smoke; it is not such a very wonderful thing to do. But a scout will not do it because he is not such a fool. He knows that when a lad smokes before he is fully grown up it is almost sure to make his heart feeble, and the heart is the most important organ in a lad's body. It pumps the blood all over him to form flesh, bone and muscle. If the heart does not do its work the body cannot grow to be healthy. Any scout knows that smoking spoils his eyesight, and also his sense of smell, which is of greatest importance to him for scouting on active service.

No boy ever began smoking because he liked it, but generally because either he feared being chaffed by the other boys as afraid to smoke, or because he thought that by smoking he would look like a great man—when all the time he only looks like a little ass.

So don't funk, but just make up your mind for yourself that you don't mean to smoke till you are grown up; and stick to it.

Drinking

A soldierly-looking man came up to me one night and brought out his discharge certificates, showing that he had served with me in South Africa. He said he could get no work, and he was starving. Every man's hand was against him, apparently because he was a soldier. My nose and eyes told me in a moment another tale, and that was the real cause of his being in distress.

A stale smell of tobacco and beer hung about his clothes, his finger-tips were yellow with cigarette smoke, he had even taken some kind of scented lozenge to try and hide the whisky smell in his breath. No wonder nobody would employ him, or give him more money to drink with, for that was all that he would do with money if he got it.

Poverty and distress are brought about by men getting into the habit of wasting their money and time on drink. And a great deal of crime, and also of illness, and even madness, is due to the same habit of drinking too much. Liquor—that is beer or spirits —is not at all necessary to make a man strong and well. Quite the contrary.

It would be simply impossible for a man who drinks to be a

scout. Keep off liquor from the very first, and make up your mind to have nothing to do with it. Water, tea or coffee are quite good enough drinks for quenching your thirst or for picking you up at any time, or, if it's very hot, lemonade or a squeeze of lemon are much better refreshment.

A good Scout trains himself pretty well to do without liquid. It is very much a matter of habit. If you keep your mouth shut when walking or running, or suck a pebble (which also makes you keep your mouth shut), you do not get thirsty like you do when you go along with your mouth open sucking in the air and dry dust. But you must also be in good hard condition. If you are fat from want of exercise, you are sure to get thirsty and want to drink every mile. If you do not let yourself drink the thirst wears off after a short time. If you keep drinking water on the line of march, or while playing games, it helps to tire you and spoils your wind.

Smile

Want of laughter means want of health. Laugh as much as you can: it does you good; so whenever you can get a good laugh, laugh on. And make other people laugh, too, when possible, as it does them good.

If you are in pain or trouble, make yourself smile at it; if you remember to do this, and force yourself, you will find it really does make a difference.

The ordinary boy is apt to frown when working hard at physical exercises, but the Boy Scout is required to smile all the time; he drops a mark off his score whenever he frowns.

CAMP FIRE YARN. No. 19

PREVENTION OF DISEASE

Microbes, and How to Fight Them

Disease is carried about in the air and in water by tiny invisible insects called "germs" or "microbes," and you are very apt to breathe them in through the mouth or to get them in your drink or food and to swallow them, and then they breed disease inside you. If your blood is in really good order, it generally does not matter, no harm results; but if your blood is out of order from weakness or constipation—that is, not going regularly to the "rear"—these microbes will very probably make you ill. A great point is, therefore, to abolish the microbes, if possible. They like living in dark, damp and dirty places. And they come from bad drains, old dustbins, and rotting flesh, etc.; in fact, generally where there is a bad smell. Therefore, keep your room, or your camp, and your clothes clean, dry and as sunny as possible, and well aired; and keep away from places that smell badly. Before your meals you should always wash your hands and finger-nails, for they are very apt to harbour microbes which have come from anything that you may have been handling in the day.

You frequently see notices in omnibuses and public places requesting you not to spit. The reason for this is that many people spit who have diseased lungs, and from their spittle the microbes of their diseases get in the air, and are breathed by healthy people into their lungs, and they become also diseased. Often you may have a disease in you for some years without knowing it, and if you spit you are liable to communicate that disease to sound people; so you should not do it for their sake.

But you need not be afraid of diseases if you breathe through your nose and keep your blood in good order. It is always well on coming out of a crowded theatre, church, or hall, to cough and blow your nose, in order to get rid of microbes which you might have breathed in from other people in the crowd. It comes very much from living in houses where the windows are kept always shut up. The best chance of getting cured of it, if you get the disease, is to sleep always out of doors.

A Scout has to sleep a great deal in the open air; therefore, when he is in a house he sleeps with the windows as wide open as possible, otherwise he feels stuffy; and also, if he gets accus-

PULLING IN A DISLOCATED SHOULDER

tomed to sleeping in a warm atmosphere he would catch cold
when he goes into camp, and nothing could be more ridiculous
or more like a tenderfoot than a Scout with a cold in his head.
When once he is accustomed to having his windows open, he
will never catch cold in a room.

Food

A good many illnesses come from over-eating or eating the
wrong kind of food. A Scout must know how to take care of
himself, else he is of no use. He must keep himself light and
active. Once he has got the right kind of muscles on, he can
remain fit without further special exercising of those muscles,
provided that he eats the right kind of food.

In the siege of Mafeking, when we were put on short commons
those of the garrison who were accustomed to eat very little at
their meals, did not suffer like some people, who had been accustomed to do themselves well in peace time; these became weak
and irritable. Our food there towards the end was limited to a
hunk of pounded-up oats, about the size of a bun, which was
our whole bread supply for the day, and about a pound of meat
and two pints of "sowens," a kind of stuff like bill-stickers' paste
that had gone wrong.

The cheapest and best foods are dried peas, flour, oatmeal, potatoes and cheese. Other good foods are fresh fruit, vegetables, fish, eggs, nuts, rice and milk, and one can live on these perfectly well without meat.

If you have lots of fresh air, you do not want much food; if, on the other hand, you are sitting indoors all day, much food makes you fat and sleepy, so that in either case you are better for taking a little; still, growing boys should not starve themselves, but, at the same time, they need not be like that little hog at the school feast, who, when asked, "Can't you eat any more?" replied, "Yes, I could *eat* more, but I've no room to *swallow* it."

Clothing

A scout's clothing should be of flannel or wool as much as possible, because it dries easily. Cotton next the skin is not good unless you change is directly it gets wet—it is so likely to give you a chill, and a scout is no use if he gets laid up.

One great point that a scout should take care about, to ensure his endurance and being able to go on the march for a long time, in his boots.

A scout who gets sore feet with much walking becomes useless.

The feet should be kept as dry as possible; if they are allowed to get wet, the skin is softened, and very soon gets blistered and rubbed raw where there is a little pressure of the boot.

Of course, they get wet from perspiration as well as from outside wet. Therefore, to dry this it is necessary to wear good woollen socks. I like shoes better than boots, because they let more air in for the feet.

If a man wears thin cotton or silk socks, you can tell at once that he is no walker. A fellow who goes overseas for the first time is called a "Tenderfoot," because he generally gets sore feet until by experience he learns how to keep his feet in good order. It is a good thing to soap or grease your feet and the inside of your socks before putting them on.

If your feet always perspire a good deal, it is a useful thing to powder them with powder made of boric acid, starch, and oxide of zinc in equal parts. This powder should be rubbed in between the toes, so as to prevent soft corns forming there. Your feet can be hardened to some extent by soaking them in alum and water, or salt and water. Wash the feet every day.

Drill for Scouts

Scouts have to drill to enable them to be moved quickly from one point to another in good order. Drill also sets them up, and makes them smart and quick.

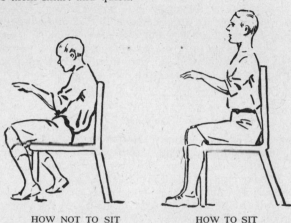

HOW NOT TO SIT   HOW TO SIT

It strengthens the muscles which support the body, and by keeping the body upright the lungs and heart get plenty of room to work, and the inside organs are kept in the proper position for proper digestion of food and so on.

A slouching position, on the other hand, depresses all the other

WALKING FOR EXERCISE

1.—The right way.   2.—A common way.
3.—A usual and very bad way.   — — — ➤ *Direction of eyes.*

ALERT   AT EASE

SECURE STAFFS
(for close order or at funerals)   SIT AT EASE   REST ON STAFFS
(At funerals)

TRAIL STAFFS   SLOPE STAFFS   SHOULDER STAFFS   SUPPORT STAFFS

SALUTES ~

WHEN MARCHING   WHEN AT "THE ALERT"   WITHOUT STAFFS

organs, and prevents them doing their work properly, so that a man in that position is generally weak and often ill.

Growing lads are very apt to slouch, and should therefore do all they can to get out of the habit by plenty of physical exercises and drill.

Stand upright when you are standing, and when you are sitting down sit upright, with your back well into the back part of the

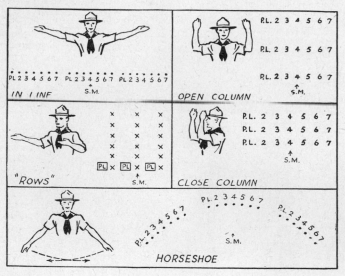

IN LINE

OPEN COLUMN

"ROWS"

CLOSE COLUMN

HORSESHOE

Drill by Signal

chair. Alertness of the body, whether you are moving, standing, or sitting, means alertness of mind, and it is a paying thing to have, because many an employer will select an alert-looking boy for work and pass over a sloucher. When you have to stoop over writing at a table, or even tying a boot-lace, do not round your back, but tuck in the small of your back, which thus helps to strengthen your body.

On the word "Alert," the Scout stands upright with both feet together, hands hanging naturally at the sides, fingers straight, and looking straight to his front.

On the word "Easy," he carries the left foot away six inches to the left, and clasps his hands behind his back, and can turn his head about. At the word "Sit easy," he squats down on the ground in any position he likes. "Sit easy" should usually be given whenever you don't want the boys to be at the "Alert," provided that the ground is dry.

On the command "Quick march," boys move off with the left foot leading at a smart pace, swinging the arms freely, as this gives good exercise to the body and muscles and inside organs.

At the command "Double," boys run at a jog-trot with short, easy steps, hands swinging loosely, not tucked up at the side.

On the command "Scout Pace" the boys march at the quick march for twenty paces, then double twenty paces, and so on, alternately running and walking, until the word is given "Quick march" or "Halt."

"Right turn," each boy turns to the right.

"Follow your leader," "Leader right turn"—the leading man turns to his right, the remainder move up to the place where he turned, and then follow after him.

"Front form line" (when "following the leader"). Those in rear run up and form in line alongside the leader on his left.

With an alert Troop movements can easily be done without any word of command; all that is needed is for the Scoutmaster to give a signal and every Scout immediately doubles to his proper place in his Patrol, the whole formation facing the Scoutmaster. For instance, for "Line" he might extend both arms straight outwards from the shoulder; for "Open column" extend both arms outwards, but bend them upwards at the elbow; for "Close column" the signal might be like that for "Open column" but with the arms held forward instead of outward from the shoulders.

Horseshoe formation is the ordinary one for Troop Parades. The signal for this is usually to swing the arms to and fro with a semi-circular motion in front of the body.

For inter-Patrol games "Rows" is used. This means that the Patrols are in Indian file, behind their Patrol Leaders with their Seconds at the back, facing the Scoutmaster, and in their usual Patrol order from right to left. The usual signal is both arms stretched forward from the shoulders.

Movements by signal are always made at the run and in dead silence.

CHIVALRY FOR OTHERS

" IN days of old, when knights were bold," it must have been a fine sight to see one of these steel-clad horsemen come riding through the dark green woods in his shining armour, with shield and lance and waving plumes, bestriding his gallant war-horse, strong to bear its load, and full of fire to charge upon an enemy. And near him rode his squire, a young man, his assistant and companion, who would some day become a knight.

Behind him rode his group or patrol of men-at-arms—stout, hearty warriors, ready to follow their knights to the gates of death if need be. They were the tough yeomen of the old days, who won so many of her fine fights for Britain through their pluck and loyal devotion to their knights.

In peace time, when there was no fighting to be done, the knight would daily ride about looking for a chance of doing a good turn to any wanting help, especially a woman or child who might be in distress. When engaged in thus doing good turns, he was called a "Knight Errant." His patrol naturally acted in the same way as their leader, and a man-at-arms was always equally

St. George

ready to help the distressed with his strong right arm. The knights of old were the Patrol Leaders of the nation, and the men-at-arms were the Scouts.

You Patrol Leaders and Scouts are therefore very like the knights and their retainers, especially if you keep your honour ever before you in the first place, and do your best to help other people who are in trouble or who want assistance. Your motto is, "Be Prepared" to do this, and the motto of the knights was a similar one, "Be Always Ready."

They had as their patron saint St. George, because he was the only one of all the saints who was a horseman. He is the patron saint of cavalry and Scouts all over Europe.

St. George is the special saint of England. The battle-cry of the knights used to be, "For Saint George and Merrie England!"

St. George's Day is April 23rd, and on that day all Scouts remind themselves of their Promise and of the Scout Law. Not that a Scout ever forgets either, but on St. George's Day he makes a special point of thinking about them. Remember this when April 23rd comes round again.

The Knights' Code

The laws of the knights were these:

"*Be always ready,* with your armour on, except when you are taking your rest at night.

Defend the poor, and help them that cannot defend themselves.

Do nothing to hurt or offend anyone else.

Be prepared to fight in the defence of England.

At whatever you are working try to win honour and a name for honesty.

Never break your promise.

Maintain the honour of your country with your life.

Rather die honest than live shamelessly.

Chivalry requireth that youth should be trained to perform the most laborious and humble offices with *cheerfulness* and grace; and to do good unto others."

These are the first rules with which the old knights started, and from which the Scout Law of to-day comes.

A knight (or Scout) is at all times a gentleman. So many people seem to think that a gentleman must have lots of money. That does not make a gentleman. A gentleman is anyone who carries out the rules of chivalry of the knights.

A London policeman, for instance, is a gentleman, because he is well disciplined, loyal, polite, brave, good-tempered, and helpful to women and children.

Unselfishness

Captain John Smith, the old English adventurer of three hundred years ago, was a pretty tough customer to deal with, as he had fought in every part of the world and had been wounded over and over again; but he also had a good, kind heart within him. He was as good a type of scout as you could find anywhere. One of his favourite expressions was, "We were born, not for ourselves, but to do good to others," and he carried this out very much in his life, for he was the most unselfish of men.

Self-Sacrifice

One of the finest examples of self-sacrifice was the action of Captain Lawrence Oates, who was on Scott's Last Expedition to the South Pole. The little party of men had reached the Pole on January 18th, 1912, and on the return journey they suffered great hardships from intense cold and terrible weather. They became weaker and weaker. One, Petty Officer Evans, died, and then Oates became badly frost-bitten in hands and feet, and he realised that he was a burden on the others. This is what Captain Scott wrote of him: "He has borne intense suffering for weeks without complaint, and to the very last was able and willing to discuss outside subjects. He did not—would not—give up hope till the very end. He was a brave soul. This was the end. He slept through the night before last, hoping not to wake; but he woke in the morning —yesterday. It was blowing a blizzard. He said, 'I am just going outside and may be some time.' He went out into the blizzard and we have not seen him since. . . . We knew that Oates was walking to his death, but though we tried to dissuade him, we knew it was the act of a brave man and an English gentleman."

Boys, too, can show just the same spirit. A lad of eighteen named Currie saw a little girl playing on the railway line at Clydebank in front of an approaching train. He tried to rescue her, but he was lame from an injury he had got at football, and it delayed him in getting her clear. The train knocked both of them over, and both were killed.

But Currie's gallant attempt is an example of chivalry for Scouts to follow. It was sacrifice of himself in the attempt to save a child.

Kindness

"Kindness and gentleness are great virtues," says an old Spanish proverb; and another says, "Oblige without regarding whom you oblige," which means be kind to anyone, great or small, rich or poor.

The great point about a knight was that he was always doing kindnesses or good turns to people. His idea was that everyone must die, but you should make up your mind that before your time comes you will do something good. Therefore do it at once, for you never know when you may be going off.

So, with the Scouts, it has been made one of our promises that we help other people at all times. It does not matter how small that good turn may be, if it only be to help an old woman lift her bundle, or to guide a child across a crowded street, or to put a halfpenny in the poor-box. Something good ought to be done each day of your life, and you should start to-day to carry out this rule, and never forget it during the remaining days of your life.

Generosity

Some people are fond of hoarding up their money and never spending it. It is well to be thrifty, but it is also well to give away money where it is wanted; in fact, that is part of the object of saving up your money. In being charitable, be careful that you do not fall into the mistake of false charity. That is to say, it is very easy and comforting to you to give a penny to a poor beggar in the street, but you ought not to do it. That poor beggar may be an arrant old fraud, and by giving your penny you are encouraging him and others to go on with that trade. There may be, probably are, hundreds of really poor and miserable people hiding away, whom you never see and to whom that penny would be a godsend.

You need not be rich in order to be charitable. Many of the knights were poor men. At one time some of them wore as their crest two knights riding on one horse, which meant that they were too poor to afford a horse apiece.

Courtesy to Women

The knights of old were particularly attentive in respect and courtesy to women.

When walking with a lady or child, a Scout should always have her on his left side, so that his right is free to protect her.

This rule is altered when walking in the streets: then a man will walk on the side of her nearest to the traffic, to protect her against accident or mud-splashes, etc.

In meeting a woman or a child a man should, as a matter of course, always make way for her, even if he has to step off the pavement into the mud.

So also in riding in a crowded bus or railway carriage, no man worthy of the name will allow a woman or a child to stand up if he has a seat. He will at once give it up to the woman and stand himself. As a Scout, you should set an example in this by being the first man in the carriage to do it. And in doing so do it cheerfully, with a smile, so that she may not think you are annoyed at having to do it.

When in the street, always be on the look-out to help women and children. A good opportunity is when they want to cross a street, or to find the way. If you see them, go and help them at once—and don't accept any reward.

You should carry your courtesy on with ladies at all times. If you are sitting down and a lady comes into the room, stand up, and see if you can help her in any way before you sit down.

Don't lark about with a girl whom you would not like your mother or sister to see you with.

Don't make love to any girl unless you mean to marry her.

Thanks!

And, look here! Here is a very important bit of courtesy that is too often forgotten, but which a true Scout will never omit, and that is *to thank* for any kindness you receive. A present is not yours till you have thanked for it. You have not finished your camp, even if you have packed up your kit and cleaned up the ground, until you have thanked the owner for use of it and have thanked God for giving you a good time.

CAMP FIRE YARN. No. 21

SELF-DISCIPLINE

Honour

THE true knight placed his honour before all things; it was sacred. A man who is honourable is always to be trusted; he will never do a dishonourable action, such as telling an untruth or deceiving his superiors or employers, or those under his orders, and always commands the respect of his fellow-men. His honour guides him in everything that he does. A captain sticks to the ship till the last, in every wreck that was ever heard of. Why? She is only a lump of iron and wood; his life is as valuable as that of any of the women and children on board, but he makes everybody get away safely before he attempts to save his more valuable life. Why? Because the ship is his ship, and he has been taught that it is his duty to stick to it, and he considers it would be dishonourable in him to do otherwise; so he puts honour before safety. So also a Scout should value his honour most of anything.

Fair Play

Britons, above all other people, insist on fair play.

If you see a big bully going for a small or weak boy, you stop him because it is not "fair play."

And if a man, in fighting another, knocks him down, he must not hit or kick him while he is down; everybody would think him an awful beast if he did. Yet there is no law about it; you could not get him imprisoned for it. The truth is that "fair play" is an old idea of chivalry that has come down to us from the knights of old, and we must always keep up that idea.

Honesty

Honesty is a form of honour. An honourable man can be trusted with any amount of money or other valuables with the certainty that he will not steal it.

Cheating at any time is a sneaking, underhand thing to do.

When you feel inclined to cheat in order to win a game, or feel very distressed when a game in which you are playing is going against you, just say to yourself, "After all, it is only a game. It won't kill me if I do lose. One can't win always, though I will stick to it in case of a chance coming."

If you keep your head in this way, you will often find that you win after all from not being over-anxious or despairing.

And don't forget, whenever you *do* lose a game, if you are a true Scout, you will at once cheer the winning team or shake hands with and congratulate the fellow who has beaten you.

This rule will be carried out in *all* games and competitions among Boy Scouts.

"O God, help me to win, but in Thy inscrutable wisdom if Thou willest me NOT to win, then, O God, make me a good loser."

Loyalty

Our highest loyalty is to God; we can show that by carrying out our duties to the Church to which we belong, and by keeping our Promise as Scouts.

Loyalty was, above all, one of the distinguishing points about the knights. They were always devotedly loyal to their Sovereign and to their country, and were always ready and eager to die in their defence. In the same way a follower of the knights should be loyal, not only to the Sovereign, but also to every one who is above him, whether his officers or employers, and he should stick to them through thick and thin as part of his duty. If he does not intend to be loyal, he will, if he has any honour and manliness in him, resign his place.

He should also be equally loyal to his own friends and should support them in evil times as well as in good times.

Loyalty to duty was shown by the Roman soldier of old who stuck to his post when the city of Pompeii was overwhelmed with ashes and lava from the volcano Vesuvius. His remains are still there, with his hand covering his mouth and nose to prevent the suffocation which in the end overcame him.

Duty Before All

General Gordon sacrificed his life to his sense of duty. When he was besieged at Khartoum he could have got away himself had he liked, but he considered it his duty to remain with the Egyptians whom he had brought there, although he had no admiration for them. So he stuck to them, and when at last the place was captured by the enemy he was killed.

Obedience and Discipline

Discipline and obedience are as important as bravery for Scouts and for soldiers.

The *Birkenhead* was a transport ship carrying troops. She had on board 630 soldiers with their families and 130 seamen. Near the Cape of Good Hope one night she ran on to some rocks, and began to break up. The soldiers were at once paraded on deck. Some were told off to get out the boats, and to put the women and children into them, and others were told off to get the horses up out of the hold, and to lower them overboard into the sea, in order that they might have a chance of swimming ashore. When this had all been done, it was found that there were not enough boats to take the men, and so the men were ordered to remain in their ranks. Then the ship broke in half and began to go down. The captain shouted to the men to jump over and save themselves, but the colonel, Colonel Seaton, said, "No, keep your ranks." For he saw that if they swam to the boats, and tried to get in, they would probably sink them too. So the men kept their ranks, and as the ship rolled over and sank, they gave a cheer and went down with her. Out of the whole 760 on board, only 192 were saved, but even those would probably have been lost had it not been for the discipline and self-sacrifice of the others.

A British training ship, the *Fort Jackson,* full of boy-sailors, was run into by a steamer, but just as in the *Birkenhead* there was no panic or crying out. The boys fell in quickly on parade, put on their lifebelts, and faced the danger calmly and well. And not a life was lost.

Humility

Humility, or being humble, was one of the things which was practised by the knights, that is to say, that, though they were generally superior to other people in fighting or campaigning, they never allowed themselves to swagger about it. So don't swagger.

And don't imagine that you have got rights in this world except those that you earn for yourself. You've got the right to be believed if you earn it by always telling the truth, and you've got the right to go to prison if you earn it by thieving; but there are lots of men who go about howling about their rights who have never done anything to earn any rights. Do your duty first, and you will get your rights afterwards.

Courage

Very few men are born brave, but any man can make himself brave if he tries—and especially if he begins trying when he is a boy.

The brave man dashes into danger without any hesitation, when a less brave man is inclined to hang back. It is very like bathing. A lot of boys will come to a river to bathe, and will cower shivering on the bank, wondering how deep the water is, and whether it is very cold—but the brave one will run through them and take his header into the water, and will be swimming about happily a few seconds later.

The thing is, when there is danger before you, don't stop and look at it—the more you look at it the less you will like it—but take the plunge, go boldly in at it, and it won't be half so bad as it looked, when you are once in it.

Fortitude

The knights were men who never said "Die" till they were dead: they were always ready to stick it out till the last extremity; but it is a very common fault with men to give in to trouble or fear long before there is any necessity. They often give up working because they don't get success all at once, and probably if they stuck to it a little longer, success would come. A man must expect hard work and want of success at first.

Some of you may have heard the story of the two frogs. If you have not, here it is:

Two frogs were out for a walk one day, and they came to a big bowl of cream. In looking into it they both fell in.

One said: "This is a new kind of water to me. How can a fellow swim in stuff like this? It is no use trying." So he sank to the bottom and was drowned through having no pluck.

But the other was a more manly frog, and he struggled to swim, using his arms and legs as hard as he could to keep himself afloat; and whenever he felt he was sinking he struggled harder than ever, and never gave up hope.

At last, just as he was getting so tired that he thought he *must* give it up, a curious thing happened. By his hard work with his arms and legs he had churned up the cream so much that he suddenly found himself standing all safe on a pat of butter!

So when things look bad just smile and sing to yourself, as the thrush sings: "Stick to it, stick to it, stick to it," and you will come through all right.

A very great step to success is to be able to stand disappointments.

Good Temper and Cheeriness

The knights laid great stress on being never out of temper. They thought it bad form to lose their temper and to show anger. Captain John Smith, of whom I spoke just now, was himself a type of a cheerful man. In fact, towards the end of his life two boys (and he was very fond of boys) to whom he told his adventures, wrote them down in a book, but they said that they found great difficulty in hearing all that he said, because he roared with laughter so over his own descriptions of his troubles. But it is very certain that had he not been a cheery man, he never could have got through half the dangers with which he was faced at different times in his career.

Over and over again he was made prisoner by his enemies—sometimes savage enemies—but he managed always to captivate them with his pleasant manner, and become friends with them, so that often they let him go, or did not trouble to catch him when he made his escape.

If you do your work cheerfully, your work becomes much more of a pleasure to you, and also if you are cheerful it makes other people cheerful as well, which is part of your duty as a Scout. Sir J. M. Barrie wrote: "Those who bring sunshine to the lives of others, cannot keep happiness from themselves," which means, if you make other people happy, you make yourself happy.

Good temper can be attained by a boy who wants to have it, and it will help him in every game under the sun, and more especially in difficulty and danger, and will often keep him in a situation where a short-tempered fellow gets turned out, or leaves in a huff.

Bad language and swearing are generally used, like smoking, by boys who want to try and show off how manly they are, but it only makes them look like fools. Generally, a man who swears is a man easily upset, who loses his head in a difficult situation, and is not, therefore, to be depended upon. You want to be quite undisturbed under the greatest difficulties; and so when you find yourself particularly anxious, or excited, or angry, don't swear, force yourself to smile, and it will set you right in a moment.

Captain John Smith, who neither smoked nor swore, had a way of dealing with swearers. He says in his diary that when his men were cutting down trees, the axes blistered their tender fingers, so that at about every third blow a loud oath would drown the echo of the axe. To remedy this he devised a plan of having every man's oath noted down, and at night, for every oath, he had a can of water poured down the wearer's sleeve, "with which an offender was so washed that a man would scarce hear an oath for a week."

SELF-IMPROVEMENT

Duty to God

A N old British chieftain, some thirteen hundred years ago, said: "Our life has always seemed to me like the flight of a sparrow through the great hall, when one is sitting at meals with the log fire blazing on the hearth, while all is storm and darkness outside. He comes in, no one knows from where, and hovers for a short time in the warmth and light, and then flies forth again into the darkness. And so it is with the life of a man; he comes no one knows from where; he is here in the world for a short time, till he flies forth again, no one knows whither. But now you show us that if we do our duty during our life we shall not fly out into darkness again, when life is ended, since Christ has opened a door for us to enter a brighter room, a heaven where we can go and dwell in peace for ever."

This old chief was speaking for all the chiefs of northern England when King Edwin had introduced to them a knowledge of the Christian religion; and they adopted it then and there as one more comforting to them than their old Pagan worship of heathen gods; and ever since those days the Christian religion has been the one to rule our country.

Religion seems a very simple thing.

1st.   Love and serve God.
2nd.   Love and serve your neighbour.

The old knights, who were the scouts of the nation, were very religious. They were always careful to attend religious service, especially before going into battle or undertaking any serious difficulty. They considered it was the right thing always to be prepared for death. In the great church of Malta you can see to-day where the old knights used to pray, and they all stood up and drew their swords during the reading of the Creed, as a sign that they were prepared to defend the gospel with their swords and lives. Besides worshipping God in church, the knights always recognised His work in the things which He made, such as animals, plants and scenery. And so it is with peace Scouts to-day, that wherever they go they love the woodlands, the mountains and the prairies, and they like to watch and know about the animals that inhabit them, and the wonders of the flowers and plants. No man is much good unless he believes in God and obeys His laws. So every Scout should have a religion.

In doing your duty to God always be grateful to Him. Whenever you enjoy a pleasure or a good game, or succeed in doing a good thing, thank Him for it, if only with a word or two, just as you say grace after a meal. And it is a good thing to bless other people. For instance, if you see a train starting off, just pray for God's blessing on all that are in the train.

In doing your duty towards man be helpful and generous, and also always be grateful for any kindness done to you, and be careful to show that you are grateful.

Remember that a present given to you is not yours until you have thanked the giver for it. While you are the sparrow flying through the hall, that is to say, while you are living your life on this earth, try and do something good which may remain after you. One writer says:

"I often think that when the sun goes down the world is hidden by a big blanket from the light of heaven, but the stars are little holes pierced in that blanket by those who have done good deeds in this world. The stars are not all the same size; some are big, some little, and some men have done great deeds and others have done small deeds, but they have made their hole in the blanket by doing good before they went to heaven."

Try and make your hole in the blanket by good work while you are on the earth.

It is something to *be* good, but it is far better to *do* good.

Thrift

It is a funny thing that out of you boys who now read these words, some of you may become rich men, many of you will be able to make comfortable homes, and some of you may die in poverty and misery. And it just depends on your own selves which you are going to do.

And you can very soon tell which your future is going to be.

The fellow who begins making money as a boy, will go on making it as a man. You may find it difficult to do at first, but it will come easier later on; but if you begin and if you go on, remember, you are pretty certain to succeed in the end—especially if you get your money by hard work.

If you only try to make it by easy means—that is by betting, say, on a football match or a horse race—you are bound to lose after a time. Nobody who makes bets ever wins in the end; it is the bookmaker, the man who receives the bets, that scores over it. Yet there are thousands of fools who go on putting their money on, because they won a bit once or hope to win some day.

Any number of poor boys have become rich men—but in nearly every case it was because they meant to do so from the first; they worked for it, and put every penny they could make into the bank to begin with.

So each one of you has the chance, if you like to take it.

The knights of old were ordered by their rules to be thrifty, that is, to save money as much as possible, not to expend large sums on their own enjoyment, but to save it in order that they might keep themselves, and not be a burden to others, and also in order that they might have more to give away in charity; and if they had no money of their own, they were not allowed to beg for it, they must work and make it in one way or another. Thus money-making goes with manliness, hard work and sobriety.

Start a money box, or better still buy National Savings stamps and then when you have say 15/- you could open a Savings Bank account or buy a National Savings Certificate. Save your pence and you will get pounds.

BE PREPARED FOR ACCIDENTS

The Knights of St. John

THE knights of old days were called "Knight Hospitallers" because they had hospitals for the treatment of the sick poor, and those injured in accidents or in war. They used to save up their money and keep these hospitals going, and although they were brave fighting men they used also to act as nurses and doctors themselves.

The Knights of St. John of Jerusalem especially devoted themselves to this work eight hundred years ago, and the St. John Ambulance Brigade is to-day a branch which represents those knights. Their badge is an eight-pointed white cross on a black ground, and when worn as an Order it has a black ribbon.

Explorers and hunters and other scouts in out-of-the-way parts of the world have to know what to do in the case of accident or sickness, either to themselves or their followers, as they are often hundreds of miles away from any doctors. For these reasons Boy Scouts should, of course, learn all they can about looking after sick people and dealing with accidents.

My brother was once camping with a friend away in the bush in Australia. His friend was drawing a cork, holding the bottle between his knees to get a better purchase. The bottle burst and the jagged edge of it ran deeply into his thigh, cutting an artery. My brother quickly got a stone, wrapped it in a handkerchief to act as a pad, and he then tied the handkerchief round the limb above the wound, so that the stone pressed on the artery. He then got a stick, and, pressing it through the loop of the handkerchief, twisted it round till the bandage was drawn so tight that it stopped the flow of blood. Had he not known what to do the man would have bled to death in a few minutes. As it was he saved his life by knowing what to do and doing it at once.

Accidents are continually happening, and Boy Scouts will continually have a chance of giving assistance at First Aid. In London alone during any one year many people have been killed and thousands injured in street accidents.

We all think a great deal of any man who, at the risk of his own life, saves someone else's.

He is a hero.

Boys especially think him so, because he seems to them to be a being altogether different from themselves. But he isn't; every boy has just as much chance of being a life-saving hero if he chooses to prepare himself for it.

It is pretty certain that nearly every one of you Scouts will some day or another be present at an accident where, if you know what to do, and do it promptly, you may win for yourself the lifelong satisfaction of having rescued or helped a fellow-creature.

Remember your motto, BE PREPARED. Be prepared for accidents by learning beforehand what you ought to do in the different kinds that are likely to occur.

Be prepared to do that thing the moment the accident does occur.

I will explain to you what ought to be done in the different kinds of accidents, and you must practise them as far as possible. But the great thing for you Scouts to bear in mind is that wherever you are, and whatever you are doing, you should think to yourself, "What accident is likely to occur here?" and, "What is my duty if it occurs?"

You are then prepared to act.

And when an accident does occur remember always that as a Scout it is your business to be the first man to go to the rescue; don't let an outsider be beforehand with you.

Suppose, for instance, that you are standing on a crowded platform at a station, waiting for the train.

You think to yourself, "Now, supposing someone falls off this platform on to the rails just as the train is coming in, what shall I do? I must jump down and jerk him off the track on to the offside into the six-foot way—there would be no time to get him up on to the platform again. Or, if the train were very close the only way would be to lie flat and make him lie flat, too, between the rails, and let the train go over us both."

Then, if this accident happened, you would at once jump down and carry out your idea, while everybody else would be running about screaming and excited and doing nothing, not knowing what to do.

Such a case actually happened. A lady fell off the platform at Finsbury Park Station just as the train was coming in; a man named Albert Hardwick jumped down and lay flat, and held her down, too, between the rails, while the train passed over both of them without touching them. The King gave him the Albert Medal for it.

CAMP FIRE YARN. No. 24

ACCIDENTS AND HOW TO DEAL WITH THEM

Panics

EVERY year numbers of lives are lost by panics, which very often are due to the smallest causes, and which might be stopped if only one or two men would keep their heads. One evening some time ago, on board a ferry-boat in New York, a man who had been catching some crabs thought it would be a good joke to let one of them loose on board the boat. This crab caught hold of the ship's cat and made it squeal, and it jumped into the middle of a crowd of school-girls, who at once scattered, screaming. This started a panic among the hundreds of passengers on board; they rushed in every direction, and in a moment the railings broke and eight people fell overboard, and before anything could be done they were swept away by the tide and drowned.

Some few years ago occurred a case of crush and panic among children in a theatre at Barnsley, from no cause at all except overcrowding, and eight children were crushed to death. More lives would certainly have been lost had not two men kept their heads and done the right thing. One man, named Gray, called to a number of the children in a cheery voice to come another way, while the man who was working a lantern-slide show threw a picture on the screen and so diverted the attention of the rest, and prevented them catching the panic. That is the great point in a panic. If only one or two men keep their heads and do the right thing on the spur of the moment, they can often calm hundreds of people, and thus save many lives.

This is a great opportunity for a Boy Scout. Force yourself to keep calm and not to lose your head. Think what is the right thing to do and do it at once.

Rescue from Fire

Instances of gallant rescues of people from burning houses are frequent. One sees them every day in the newspapers, and Scouts should study each of these cases as they occur, and imagine to themselves what they would have done under the circumstances, and in this way you begin to learn how to deal with the different accidents.

House on Fire !

If you discover a house on fire you should act according to the following directions : —

1st—Alarm the people inside.

2nd—Warn the nearest policeman or fire-brigade station.

3rd—Rouse neighbours to bring ladders, mattresses, carpets, to catch people jumping.

After arrival of fire engines the best thing boys can do is to help the police in keeping back the crowd out of the way of the firemen, hose, etc.

There is a useful kind of drill called "Scrum" for keeping back the crowd. The Scouts form a line, or double line, and pass their arms round each other's waists, and shove, head down, into the crowd, and so drive it back.

If it is necessary to go into a house to search for feeble or insensible people, the thing to do is to place a wet handkerchief or cloth over your nose and mouth and walk in a stooping position, or crawl along on your hands and knees quite near the floor, as it is here that there is least smoke or gas. Also, for passing through fire and sparks, if you can, get hold of a blanket, and wet it, and cut a hole in the middle through which to put your head; it forms a kind of fireproof mantle, with which you can push through flames and sparks.

When a fire occurs anywhere near, the Boy Scouts should assemble their Patrols as quickly as possible and go off at scout pace to the fire, guided by the glare or the smoke. Then the Patrol Leader should report to the police or firemen, and offer the help of his Patrol either to form a fence to keep the crowd back, or to run messages, or guard property, or to help in any way.

If you find a person with his clothes on fire, you should throw him flat on the floor, because flames only burn upwards, then roll him up in the hearthrug or carpet, coat or blanket, and take care in doing so that you don't catch fire yourself. The reason for doing this is that fire cannot continue to burn where it has no air.

HOW TO HAUL AN INSENSIBLE PERSON OUT OF DANGER

When you find an insensible person, and very often in their fright they will have hidden themselves under beds and tables, etc., you should either carry him out on your shoulder, or, what is often more practicable in the case of heavy smoke, gas fumes, or in battle when under heavy fire, etc., harness yourself on to him with sheets or cords and drag him out of the room along the floor, crawling on all fours yourself.

To do this you make a bowline at each end of your rope, one you put over the patient's chest and under his arms, and the other over your own neck, then with your back to his head you start on "all fours" to pull him along head first. If the bowline is the right length it will keep his head up off the ground, as the picture on page 160 shows.

Rescue from Drowning

The list of Boy Scout heroes shows you what a large proportion of accidents are due to not knowing how to swim. It is therefore most important that everybody should learn to swim, and, having done so, to learn how to save others from being drowned.

A moderate swimmer can save a drowning man if he knows how, and has practised it a few times with his friends. The popular idea that a drowning person rises three times before he finally sinks is all nonsense. He often drowns at once, unless someone is quick to help him. The important point is not to let the drowning person catch hold of you, or he will probably drown you too. Keep behind him always. If you find yourself clutched by the wrist, turn your wrist against his thumb and force yourself free. Your best way in helping a drowning man is to keep behind and hold him up by the elbows, or by the back of the neck, or by putting your arms under his armpits and your hands across his chest, and telling him to keep quiet and not to struggle. If he obeys, you can easily keep him afloat; but otherwise be careful that in his terror he does not turn over and catch hold of you. If he should seize you by the neck, place your arm round his waist, and the other hand, palm upwards, under his chin, with your finger-tips under his nose, pull and push with all your might, and he must perforce let go. But you will never remember this unless you practise it frequently with other boys first, each taking it in turns to be the drowning man or rescuer.

No Scout can be of real use till he can swim, and to learn swimming is no more difficult than to learn bicycling.

All you have to do is at first to try and swim like a dog, as if trying to crawl slowly along in the water; don't try all at once to swim with the ordinary breast stroke that swimmers use, because this only lets your mouth go under water every time. When paddling along like a dog get a friend to support you at first with a pole or his hand under your belly.

Any of you who cannot swim as yet, and who fall into the water out of your depth, remember that you need not sink if you take care to do the following things. First, keep your mouth upwards by throwing the head well back. Secondly, keep your lungs full of air by taking in long breaths, but breathe out very little. Thirdly, keep your arms under water. To do this you should not begin to shout, which will only empty your lungs, and you should not throw your arms about or beckon for help, else you will sink.

If you see a person fall into the water and begin to drown, and you yourself are unable to swim, you must throw a rope, or an oar, or plank right over him, so that when he comes up again he may clutch at it and hold it. If a person falls through ice, and is unable to get out again because of the edges breaking, throw him a rope and tell him not to struggle. This may give him confidence until you can get a long ladder or pole across the hole, which will enable him to crawl out, or will allow you to crawl out to catch hold of him.

CAMP FIRE YARN. No. 25

RENDERING FIRST AID

Helping Others

WARNING.—You are not a doctor; as a First Aider you should send for a doctor at once except for minor cuts, etc. Your job is to prevent the patient from getting worse before medical attention can arrive. Of course, if there is no possibility of getting a doctor, then you must do the best you can.

In an accident when you are alone with the injured person, if he is unconscious lay him on his back with his head a little raised and on one side so that he does not choke, and so that any vomit or water, etc., can run out of his mouth. Loosen the clothing about his neck and chest. See where he is injured and treat him according to what you are taught in learning "First Aid."

If you have found the man lying insensible you should carefully examine the ground round him for any "sign," and take note of it and of his position, etc., in case it should afterwards appear that he had been attacked by others.

If you are out with a Patrol and an accident happens, or you find an injured man, a Patrol Leader should direct one Scout to go for a doctor, he himself will attend to the patient with one Scout to help him. The Second will use the other Scouts in assisting by getting water or blankets, or making a stretcher, or keeping the crowd back by forming a fence with their staffs.

As a rule it is best to keep the patient quite quiet at first; unless it is necessary, do not try to move him; and don't bother him with questions until he recovers a bit.

ARTIFICIAL RESPIRATION.—To restore anyone who is apparently drowned, it is necessary at once to clear the water out of his lungs, for which purpose therefore you should incline him face downwards and head downwards, so that the water may run out of his mouth, and to help it you should open his mouth and pull forward his tongue. After running the water out of the patient, place him on his side with his body slightly hanging down, and keep the tongue hanging out. If he is breathing, let him rest; if he is not breathing, you must at once endeavour to restore breathing artificially.

How TO REVIVE A DROWNED MAN.—There are several methods but the simplest is, I think, that called after its inventor, the Schäfer system. It consists merely in laying the patient on his front, and then squeezing the air out of him and letting it run in again.

1. Immediately after the removal from the water, and before taking time to loosen clothing, etc., lay the patient face downwards, with arms extended and the face turned to the side. Kneel or squat alongside or astride of the patient, facing towards his head.

2. Place your hands on the small of the patient's back, one on each side, with thumbs parallel and nearly touching, and the fingers reaching only to the lowest ribs.

3. Swing forward with the arms straight, so as to allow the weight of your body to fall on your wrists, and then make a firm, steady downward pressure on the loins of the patient, while you count slowly in thousands—"one thousand, two thousand"—to press the patient's stomach against the ground and to force the air from his chest.

4. Then swing your body backwards so as to relieve the pressure, and without removing your hands, while you count slowly, "three thousand, four thousand, five thousand."

Continue this backward and forward movement, alternately relieving and pressing the patient's stomach against the ground in order to drive the air out of his chest and mouth, and allowing it to suck itself in again, until gradually the patient begins to do it for himself.

The proper pace for the movement should be about twelve pressures to the minute.

As soon as the patient is breathing, you can leave off the pressure; but watch him, and if he fails you must start again till he can breathe for himself; it may be necessary to have relays of helpers.

Then let him lie in a natural position, and set to work to get him warm by putting hot flannels or bottles of hot water between his thighs and under the arms, and against the soles of his feet.

Wet clothing should be taken off and hot blankets rolled round him. The patient should be disturbed as little as possible, and encouraged to sleep, while carefully watched for at least an hour afterwards.

Now just practise this with another Scout a few times, so that you understand exactly how to do it, and so Be Prepared to do it to some poor fellow, maybe, really in need of it, one day.

ACID BURNING.—A case occurred of a woman throwing vitriol over a man's face. This is an awful acid, which burns and eats away the flesh wherever it touches. Fortunately a policeman happened to be on the spot at the time, and knew what to do. He at once applied half-warm water to which some soda had been added to wash off the acid, and then applied flour or whitening to protect the wound from the air and ease the pain as you would do for a burn.

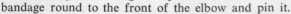

BANDAGE.—For binding a broken limb you want a good large three-cornered bandage. Its two sides should be each about forty inches long.

To make a large arm-sling, hang the bandage round the patient's neck with the point of the bandage towards the damaged arm, and tie the two ends together in a reef-knot on the injured side. Rest the arm in this sling and bring the point of the bandage round to the front of the elbow and pin it.

BLEEDING.—When a man is bleeding badly from an artery, press the wound or the flesh just above it—that is, between the wound and the heart—press it hard with your thumb to try and stop the blood running in the artery. Then make a pad with something like a flat, rounded pebble, and bind it over the wound. If bleeding violently, lay the patient flat on the ground, keep the wounded part raised above the rest of the body if possible (but not, of course, if the wound is in a broken limb), wrap warmly and treat for shock.

Bleeding from the ears and insensibility after a fall mean injury to the skull. The patient should not be moved at all if possible. It is best even to keep him lying on the spot, and put cold water or ice to his head and keep him quiet till a doctor comes.

Spitting or throwing up blood means internal injury or bursting of a small blood-vessel inside the patient. The case often looks more serious than it really is. If the blood is light red in colour and mixed with froth, it means injury to the lungs. In either case lay the patient down and keep him quiet; if he is bleeding from the lungs, you may give ice to suck or cold water to sip, but otherwise do not give anything at all by the mouth to a patient with internal bleeding.

Don't be alarmed at the amount of blood that flows from a patient. It used to be a common thing for the barber to bleed a man to the extent of five or six cupfuls of blood.

BLOOD-POISONING.—This results from dirt being allowed to get into a wound. Swelling, pain, red veins appear. Fomenting with hot water is the best relief.

BROKEN LIMBS.—How to tell when a limb is broken.

There is generally a swelling and pain about the place where the bone is broken, and sometimes the limb is bent in an unnatural way and the patient cannot use it.

The broken limb should not be moved about at all, but should be straightened and bound to something stiff that will keep it stiff and straight while the patient is being moved to hospital or home.

BURNS.—In all cases of severe burns or scalds send for the doctor at once, and treat the patient for shock—that is, lay him down as comfortably as possible and wrap him up warmly with blankets and hot bottles.

Do NOT pull charred or sticking clothing off a severe burn or scald, do NOT break blisters, and do NOT put on any sort of an oily dressing.

For a small burn Tannic Acid Jelly (sold in tubes by all chemists) smeared thickly over the skin and allowed to dry before a dressing is applied, is the best treatment. For more severe burns or scalds, cover the area with clean lint (smooth side next the skin, fluffy side outwards) or surgical gauze, or with the inner surface of a clean white handkerchief straight from the wash, bandage firmly (or lightly if blisters have formed), and if there is delay in getting the patient to doctor or hospital, soak the whole of the dressing and bandage in a solution of bicarbonate of soda (two teaspoonfuls to a pint of warm water) or common salt (one teaspoonful to a pint).

CHOKING.—To dislodge the obstruction, lean the patient forward and thump the back hard between the shoulder-blades. A child may be turned upside down and thumped on the back. If this is unsuccessful, open the mouth, forcibly if need be, pass two fingers along the tongue right to the back of the throat and try to pull up the foreign body. If this is impossible, push it back into the gullet. If vomiting results, immediately turn the head on one side.

Choking sometimes comes from a sudden swelling inside the throat. In this case put hot steaming flannel fomentations to the neck and give the patient ice to suck or cold water to sip.

CONCUSSION or STUNNING is a common result of a fall or bang on the head.

The worst thing you can do is to give spirits or stimulants and to move the patient. Keep him quite still in a darkened room if available. He should be lying flat with head on one side. Treat for shock, i.e., warmth applied to sides and feet (blankets, hot-water bottle, etc.). As concussion may be very serious, a doctor must be obtained as soon as possible.

ELECTRIC SHOCK.—Men frequently get knocked insensible by touching an electric cable or rail. The patient should be moved from the rail, but you have to be careful in doing this that you don't get the electric shock also. If possible, switch off electric current. In the first place put glass, if possible, for yourself to stand upon, or dry wood if glass is not obtainable, or put on india-rubber boots. Also put on india-rubber gloves before touching the patient. If you have none, wrap your hands in several thicknesses of *dry* cloth, and pull the patient away with a dry wooden object, e.g., staff, broom, etc.

Artificial respiration may be necessary; when breathing is restored, treat for shock.

A boy was hunting butterflies at St. Ouen, in France, when he fell on the "live" rail of the electric railway and was instantly killed by the shock. A passer-by, in trying to lift him off, fell dead beside him. A brickmaker ran up and tried to rescue them and was himself struck dead in the same way. The two would-be rescuers were killed through not having learned beforehand what was the right thing to do.

FAINTING.—Loosen all tight clothing, and keep the patient in a reclining position. If the face is pale, keep the head low and elevate the limbs. Extra warmth should be applied. Give smelling-salts.

Give the patient plenty of air. Give no stimulants.

FISH-HOOK IN THE SKIN.—I got a fish-hook into my finger the other day. I got a knife and cut off all the fly which was on the hook, then pushed the hook farther into my finger till the point began to push against the skin from inside. With a sharp knife I cut a little slit in the skin so that the point came easily through, and I was then able to get hold of it and to pull the whole hook through. Of course you cannot get a hook out backwards, as the barb holds tight in the flesh all the time. Clean the wound.

FITS.—A man cries out and falls, and twitches and jerks his limbs about, froths at the mouth : he is in a fit. It is no good to do anything to him but to put a bit of wood or cork between his jaws, so that he does not bite his tongue. Undo any tight clothing, and give him fresh air. Let him sleep well after a fit.

GRIT IN THE EYE.—Do not let your patient rub the eye; it will only cause inflammation and swelling, and so make the difficulty of removing the grit all the greater.

If the grit is in the lower eyelid, draw down the lid as far as you can, and gently brush it out with the corner of a moistened handkerchief, or with a paint-brush, or feather.

If it is under the upper lid, pull the lid away from the eyeball, and push the under lid up underneath the upper one. In this way the eyelashes of the lower lid will generally clean the inside of the upper one.

Another way, which every Scout must practise, is to seat your patient and stand behind him yourself with the back of his head against your chest. Lay a card, match, or any flat substance under your own thumb on the upper part of the upper eyelid, and then catch hold of the edge of the eyelid and draw it upwards over the match so that it turns inside out; gently remove the grit with a feather or wet handkerchief, and roll the eyelid down again.

If the eye is much inflamed, bathe it with lukewarm water.

If the grit is firmly imbedded in the eye, drop a little oil (olive or castor oil) into the lower lid; close the eye, and bandage it with a soft wet pad and bandage, and get a doctor to see it.

Remember that the eye is a delicate organ and care should be taken in removing a foreign body.

HYSTERICS.—Nervous people, especially women, get hysterics when excited, crying, laughing and screaming. The best treatment is to shut the patient into a room and leave him entirely alone till he gets over it. Don't try and soothe him, it only makes him worse.

POISONING.—If a person suddenly falls very ill after taking food, or is known to have taken poison, the first thing to do is to send for a doctor. Then, if the mouth is not stained or burnt by the poison, make him sick if possible by giving him salt or mustard and warm water, and try tickling the inside of his throat with a feather. Then give him a soothing drink such as barley water, salad oil, or flour and water. If the poison is an acid that burns, the patient should not be made to vomit, but give magnesia, or baking soda, or whitening to destroy the acid. The patient should be kept awake if he gets drowsy. A Scout will notice any bottle or other clue which may tell the doctor the nature of the poison, and any remains of food should be kept.

SMOKE OR FUMES.—Accidents are continually occurring from escapes of gas in mines, sewers, and houses.

In endeavouring to rescue a person, keep your nose and mouth well covered with a wet handkerchief, and get your head as close to the floor as possible, and drag the insensible person out as I have suggested in case of a fire. Drag your patient as quickly as possible into the fresh air—(I say as quickly as possible, because if you delay about it you are very apt to be overcome by the noxious gas yourself)—then loosen all his clothing about the neck and chest, dash cold water in his face, and apply burnt feathers under his nose. If you find that he is no longer breathing, then treat him as you would a drowned person, and try and work back the breath into his body.

SPLINTS.—The stiff thing that you tie to the injured limb is called a splint. This may be anything, such as a wooden batten, Scout's staff, tightly rolled newspaper, etc.

Splints should be long enough to go beyond the joints above and below the break. You should put a splint on each side of the limb if possible.

Then bind the splints firmly from end to end with handkerchiefs or strips of linen or cloths, but not so tightly as to stop the blood circulating or to press into the swelling. Tie with reef knots.

SNAKE BITE.—Fortunately poisonous snakes are uncommon in England, but if you travel abroad you may come across them, and you ought always to know how to deal with bites from them. The same treatment does also for wounds from poisoned arrows, mad dogs, etc. Remember the poison from a bite gets into your blood, and goes all through your body in a very few beats of your pulse. Therefore, whatever you do must be done immediately. The great thing is to stop the poison rushing up the veins into the body. To do this bind a cord or handkerchief immediately round the limb *above* the place where the patient has been bitten, so as to stop the blood flying back to the heart with the poison. Then try and suck the poison out of the wound, but spit out the poison at once, and, if possible, cut the wound still more, to make it bleed, and run the poison out. The poison, when sucked into the mouth, does no harm unless you have a wound in your mouth. Crystals of potassium permanganate should be rubbed into the bite. The patient should also be given stimulants, such as coffee or spirits, to a very big extent, and not allowed to become drowsy, but should be walked about and pricked and smacked in order to keep his senses alive.

STINGS.—A bee leaves its sting in the wound, so remove it with tweezers or a clean needle. The best antidote for all stings is ammonia. Failing this use bicarbonate of soda. Cold compresses can be placed on any swelling.

Suicides

Where a man has gone so far as to attempt suicide, a Scout should know what to do with him. In the case of a man cutting his throat, the great point is to stop the bleeding from the artery, if it be cut. The artery runs from where the collar-bone and breast-bone join up, to the corner of the jaw, and the way to stop bleeding is to press hard with the thumb on the side of the wound nearest to the heart, and pressure should be kept as hard as possible until assistance arrives. In a case where the would-be suicide has taken poison, make him vomit (unless it is an acid poison), which is done by tickling the inside of the throat with the finger or a feather, or pouring down his throat a tumbler of water mixed with a tablespoonful of mustard or salt.

In the case of hanging, cut down the body at once, taking care to support it with one arm while cutting the cord. Cut the noose, loosen all tight clothing about the neck and chest. Let the patient have as much fresh air as possible, throw cold water on the face and chest, or cold and hot water alternately. Perform artificial breathing, as in the case of apparently drowned people.

A tenderfoot is sometimes inclined to be timid about handling an insensible man or a dead man or even of seeing blood. Well, he won't be much use till he gets over such nonsense; the poor insensible fellow can't hurt him, and he must force himself to catch hold of him; when once he has done this his fears will pass off.

How to Carry a Patient

To Carry an Injured Person.—A four-handed seat can be made by two Scouts each grasping his left wrist with his right hand and in the same way grasping the right wrist of the other

FOUR-HANDED SEAT   THREE-HANDED SEAT WITH ARM REST

Scout with his left hand. If a back is required a three-handed seat is made in much the same way, except that one Scout makes a back by grasping the arm of the other.

STRETCHERS may be arranged in some of the following ways:

(a) A hurdle, shutter, door, gate, covered well with straw, hay, clothing, sacking.

(b) A piece of carpet, blanket, sacking, tarpaulin, spread out; and two stout poles rolled up in the sides. Put clothes for a pillow.

(c) Two coats, with the sleeves turned inside out; pass two poles through the sleeves; button the coats over them.

(d) Two poles passed through a couple of sacks, through holes at the bottom corners of each.

In carrying a patient on a stretcher be careful that he is made quite comfortable before you start. Let both bearers rise together; they must walk *out of step,* and take short paces. It should be the duty of the hinder bearer to keep a careful watch on the patient.

If the poles are short four bearers will be necessary, one at each corner of the stretcher.

CAMP FIRE YARN. No. 26

OUR COUNTRY

IN the first of these yarns I said, "I suppose every boy wants to help his country in some way or other." It's not enough to *want* to help, you must know *how* to help, and I hope that by this you have learnt quite a lot of things that you will find useful in making yourself helpful to your country.

For instance, you should by now be more observant, be able to look after yourself, know how to help people in difficulties or in accidents; you should have learnt how to obey orders quickly— and when necessary *how* to give them as well. You see, a country is made up of the individuals in it, and if each of them trains himself to be useful and to think of others and not merely of himself, then the country as a whole will be a finer one than ever.

Just as you should not want to be healthier and cleverer for your own sake alone, so we want our country to be the best possible so that it can have a good influence on others.

First we must be good citizens and firm friends all round among ourselves, because a house divided against itself cannot stand.

For this you must begin, as boys, to look on all classes of boys as your friends. Remember, whether rich or poor, from town or from country, you are all Britons in the first place, and you've got to continue to make Britain a power for good in the world. You have to stand shoulder to shoulder to do it.

If you are divided among yourselves you are doing harm to your country. You must sink your differences.

If you despise other boys because they belong to a poorer home than yourself you are a snob; if you hate other boys because they happen to be born richer and belong to more expensive schools than yourself you are a fool.

We have got, each one of us, to take our place as we find it in this world and make the best of it, and pull together with the others around us.

We are very much like bricks in a wall, we have each our place, though it may seem a small one in so big a wall. But if one brick gets rotten, or slips out of place, it begins to throw an undue strain on others, cracks appear, and the wall totters.

Try and prepare yourself for this by seriously taking up the subjects they teach you at school, not because it amuses you, but because it is your duty to your country to improve yourself. Take up your mathematics, your history, and your language learning in that spirit, and you'll get on.

Don't think of yourself, but think of your country, and your employer, and the good that your work is going to do to other people.

I hope that as a Scout you no longer take everything for granted but ask yourself the Whys and Wherefores of things.

Take that policeman. Why is he there? Who put him there? How did we come to have policemen?

Or that public swimming bath in which you get such a lot of fun, who owns it? Where did the money come from? Who pays to keep it going?

So we can go on asking question after question, and the answer will often be, "The Government," or "The Council." Now what you have to remember is that "The Government," or "The Council" is not something put over us, but something elected by the "grown-ups," and if things go wrong, or if bad things are not put right, or injustices neglected, then "The Government," or "The Council" can be changed if enough people decide that the time has come for a change.

Our Government

Of all the different kinds of government in the world, ours is the easiest and fairest for everybody.

Some countries have dictators who make their laws for them, whether the people like the laws or not; other countries make their own laws but have not a king or a queen or a head who can carry on dealings on equal terms with other foreign countries.

With us the wants of the people are remedied through Parliament. The House of Commons is made up of men chosen by the people to make known their wants and to suggest remedies, and the House of Lords sees whether these are equally good for all and for the future of the country; and what they recommend the Queen makes into law.

When you grow up you will become voters and have a share in putting members into the House of Commons.

And you will many of you be inclined to belong to Conservative or Liberal or Labour or other parties, whichever your father or friends belong to. I should not, if I were you. I should hear what each party has to say. If you listen to one party you will certainly agree that that is the only right one, the rest must all be wrong. But if you go and listen to another you will find that after all that one is quite right, and the first one wrong.

The thing is to listen to them all, and don't be persuaded by any particular one. And then be a man, make up your mind and decide for yourself which you think is best for the country—not for some twopenny-halfpenny little local question—and vote for that one so long as it works the right way, namely, for the good of the country.

CAMP FIRE YARN. No. 27

OUR COMMONWEALTH AND EMPIRE

SHOPPING for mother may seem at times rather dull, but if you keep your eyes open it can be quite a romantic tour of the Empire. Here is a list of some things and where they come from: oranges from South Africa, pineapples from Malaya, bananas from Jamaica, sugar from the West Indies or Mauritius, cocoa from Trinidad or West Africa, tea from Ceylon, India or Pakistan, coffee from Kenya, or grapefruit from Honduras.

Do you know where all those places are? Look them up on the map and you will find that they are all British, and they are scattered all over the world.

Nations of the Commonwealth

The British countries vary in size and population. Thus India and Pakistan together have an area of 862,599 square miles and a population of over 250 millions (England and Wales and Scotland together have an area of about 89,000 square miles and a population of 45 millions). Then at the other extreme is Ascension with an area of 38 square miles and 200 inhabitants!

They vary, too, in the way in which they are governed. First come the great Nations of the Commonwealth with their own Parliaments. They are so completely under their own management that each declared for itself the accession of Queen Elizabeth II to the throne; they didn't even do it all on the same day!

The Nations of the Commonwealth are the following:

Canada.
Australia.
New Zealand.
Union of South Africa.
India.
Pakistan.
Ceylon.

The Colonial Empire

In addition to the Nations of the Commonwealth there are many other British countries which do not entirely govern themselves; how far they do so depends on many things—for instance, the stage of education reached by the inhabitants. But all of them—and this is the point to remember—are on the way to self-government. Some are farther on the road than others, but all will sooner or later take charge of their own affairs.

We no longer think of the colonies as places made for our special benefit or profit; in the past many mistakes have been made, but that is how we have had to learn the duty of being in charge of these colonies. The first consideration now is, how can we best help the peoples—whatever their colours—who live in these places?

A good example of how countries have developed under our rule is Ashanti, on the West Coast of Africa. I was out there in 1895, when we marched into Ashanti and stopped the slave-dealing and the horrible sacrifices which went on. It was little better than a savage country then. Yet in 1924, at the Wembley Empire Jamboree, there were Scouts from Ashanti who brought me messages from their fathers who had served under me nearly thirty years previously. I was interested to find that they remembered me as "Kantankye," which means "He of the Big Hat," because even then I used to wear a Scout Hat. Now the Ashantis are being educated along their own lines, and have become a happy, prosperous people. Tribe no longer fears tribe.

Perhaps some day you may have a chance of helping in the training of such people; you will then find your Scouting of great value, for you have learnt to make no difference between one Scout and another, whatever his creed or colour. If you are looking for an interesting life, let me suggest you find out what possibilities there are for you in the various colonial services; it may mean hard work to get such a job, but I am sure you will never regret that, once you win the chance of doing some of the most fascinating work in the world.

John Smith

I wish I had time to tell you the story of how we came to have this Empire. It is a wonderful tale of adventure and romance, and some of the finest characters in British history have played their parts in it. For instance, think of the men who crossed the Atlantic to colonise America.

It took Sir Walter Raleigh, Captain John Smith, and other great pioneers four or five months to get there in their little cockle-shells of ships, some of them only 30 tons measurement—no bigger than a Thames barge. Nowadays you can get there in five or six days, instead of months, in steamers of 50,000 tons.

Think of the pluck of those men tackling a voyage like that, with very limited supply of water and salt food. And, when they got to land with their handful of men, they had to overcome the savages, and in some cases other Europeans, like the Dutch, the Spaniards, and the French; and then they had hard work to till the ground, to build settlements, and to start commerce.

Hard sailoring, hard soldiering, hard colonising by those old British sea-dogs, Sir Francis Drake, Sir Walter Raleigh, Hawkins, Frobisher, and, best of all to my mind, Captain John Smith.

He left Louth Grammar School in Lincolnshire to become a clerk in an office, but he soon went off to the wars. After two years' fighting he returned home.

He admitted he had gone out as a "tenderfoot," and had not properly prepared himself as a boy for a life of adventure; so he set to work then and there to learn Scouting. He built himself a hut in the woods, and learned stalking game, and killing and cooking it for himself; he learned to read maps and to draw them, and also the use of weapons; and then, when he had made himself really good at scoutcraft, he went off to the wars again.

He afterwards became a sailor, fought in some very tough sea-fights, and eventually, in 1607, he went with an expedition to colonise Virginia in America. They sailed from London in three ships, the biggest of which was only 100 tons, the smallest 30 tons. But they got there after five months, and started a settlement on the James River.

Here John Smith was captured by the Red Indians one day when out shooting, and they were proceeding to kill him when the King's daughter, Pocahontas, asked for him to be spared. After this the Red Indians and the Whites got on good terms with each other. Pocahontas became a Christian, and married Smith's lieutenant, Rolfe, and came to England. After many strange and exciting adventures in America, John Smith got much damaged by an accidental explosion of gunpowder, and came home ill. He eventually died in London.

OUR WORLD-WIDE BROTHERHOOD

THE Boy Scout and Girl Guide Movements have spread all over the world. In July 1939, there were over three million Boy Scouts in some fifty different countries. So if you become a Scout you join a great host of boys of many nationalities and you will have friends in every continent. The number is not, alas, as great as it might be, for some countries have banned Scouts simply because they did not fit into the political scheme of the rulers.

The Jamborees

We can look back, though, to considerable progress in the years before 1939. A series of Jamborees, and other meetings of Scouts from many countries, showed what a firm link the Scout Law is between boys of all colours, races and creeds. We can camp together, go hiking together, and enjoy all the fun of outdoor life, and so help to forge a chain of friendship and not of bondage.

At each of these Jamborees it has been my privilege to try to sum up the message of the meeting at a final rally. I want to repeat here some of the things I said.

In 1920 the Jamboree was at Olympia, in London. As Chief Scout of the World, I said : —

"Brother Scouts, I ask you to make a solemn choice. Differences exist between the peoples of the world in thought and sentiment, just as they do in language and physique. The War has taught us that if one nation tries to impose its particular will upon others cruel reaction is bound to follow. The Jamboree has taught us that if we exercise mutual forbearance and give and take, then there is sympathy and harmony. If it be your will, let us go forth from here fully determined that we will develop among ourselves and our boys that comradeship, through the world-wide spirit of the Scout Brotherhood, so that we may help to develop peace and happiness in the world and goodwill among men. Brother Scouts, answer me. Will you join in this endeavour?"

In 1929 we celebrated our Coming-of-Age; it was 21 years since the first edition of this book had appeared; what had been an acorn had grown into a mighty oak. The Jamboree was held at Arrowe Park, near Birkenhead. The name  of the place suggested that a good symbol of this meeting of Scouts from 41 nations and from 31 parts of the Empire, would be a Golden Arrow. At the final Rally I therefore handed to the various contingents these symbols, and in doing so I used these words: —

"From all corners of the earth you have journeyed to this great gathering of World Fellowship and Brotherhood. To-day I send you out from Arrowe to all the world, bearing my symbol of Peace and Fellowship, each one of you my ambassador, bearing my message of Love and Fellowship on the wings of Sacrifice and Service, to the ends of the earth. From now on the Scout Symbol of peace is the Golden Arrow. Carry it fast and far that all men may know the Brotherhood of Man."

Four years later we met at Gödöllö, in Hungary. The symbol for this time was a White Stag. My message was:

"You may look on the White Stag as the pure spirit of Scouting, springing forward and upward, ever leading you onward and upward to leap over difficul-

ties, to face new adventures in your active pursuit of the higher
aims of Scouting—aims which bring you happiness. Those aims
are your duty to God, to your country, and to your fellow
men, by carrying out the Scout Law. In that way, you will each
one of you, bring about God's kingdom upon earth—the reign
of peace and goodwill.

"Therefore, before leaving you, I ask you Scouts this question
—Will you do your best to make
friends with others and peace in the
world?"

Then came the Jamboree in
Holland in 1937. The symbol then
was the Jacob's Staff which mariners
used in olden times in navigation.
We little knew then what agony was
to come to that gallant country and
to many others before many years
passed. At the final rally I said:—

"This brotherhood of Scouting
is in many respects similar to a
Crusade. You Scouts have assembled from all parts of the world
as ambassadors of good will, and you have been making friends,
breaking down any barriers of race, of creed, or of class. That
surely is a great Crusade. I advise you now to continue that good
work, for soon you will be men, and if quarrels should arise
between any nations it is upon you that the burden of responsibility will fall.

"If you are friends you will not want to be in dispute, and by
cultivating these friendships such as have been cemented at this
great Jamboree, you are preparing the way for solutions of inter-
national problems by discussion of a peaceful character. This
will have a vital and very far-reaching effect throughout the
world in the cause of peace, and so pledge all of you here in this
great assembly of Youth, to do your absolute utmost to establish
friendship among Scouts of all nations."

The Coming of War

When war came in September, 1939, it looked at first as though
we had failed. But there was another side of the picture. The
wonderful way in which all members of the Boy Scouts offered
themselves for service to their countries; the courage shown even
by the youngest, and the heroism displayed by many a boy, give

us hope. If only the same spirit can animate us during peace, we can face the future with confidence.

It is the spirit that matters. Our Scout Law and Promise, *when we really put them into practice,* take away all occasion for wars and strife between nations.

So let us all do our part. Those who are Scouts now should determine to be better Scouts, not only in backwoodsmanship and camping, but in sticking to the Law and carrying it out. If you are not a Scout, come along and join this happy Brotherhood; there are great times ahead, and we shall need you!

Finally

I hope I have been able in this book to show you something of the appeal that lies in Scouting for all of us. I want you to feel that you are really Scouts out in the wilds, able to work things out for yourselves, and not just Scouts in a Troop carefully looked after by Patrol Leaders and Scouters. I know that you want to be up and doing things for yourselves; that these old explorers and frontiersmen appeal to the spirit of adventure in you; that, despite all the modern inventions of the cinema, wireless, motor-bicycles, etc., you want to get out on your own, fending for yourselves, pitting yourselves against the forces of nature, exercising yourselves with games, enjoying the freedom of the open air.

I have just tried to suggest to you some ways of doing this and of helping yourselves to become real men.

Scouting is a fine game, if we put our backs into it and tackle it well; and no game is any good to anyone unless he works up some kind of enthusiasm about it. As with other games, too, we will find that we gain strength of body, mind, and spirit from the playing of it. But remember! it is a game for the open air, so whenever the opportunity occurs get out into the open, and good luck and good camping go with you.

THE LAST MESSAGE

Dear Scouts,—If you have ever seen the play "Peter Pan" you will remember how the pirate chief was always making his dying speech because he was afraid that possibly when the time came for him to die he might not have time to get it off his chest. It is much the same with me, and so, although I am not at this moment dying, I shall be doing so one of these days and I want to send you a parting word of good-bye.

Remember, it is the last you will ever hear from me, so think it over.

I have had a most happy life and I want each one of you to have as happy a life too.

I believe that God put us in this jolly world to be happy and enjoy life. Happiness doesn't come from being rich, nor merely from being successful in your career, nor by self-indulgence. One step towards happiness is to make yourself healthy and strong while you are a boy, so that you can be useful and so can enjoy life when you are a man.

Nature study will show you how full of beautiful and wonderful things God has made the world for you to enjoy. Be contented with what you have got and make the best of it. Look on the bright side of things instead of the gloomy one.

But the real way to get happiness is by giving out happiness to other people. Try and leave this world a little better than you found it and when your turn comes to die, you can die happy in feeling that at any rate you have not wasted your time but have done your best. "Be Prepared" in this way, to live happy and to die happy—stick to your Scout Promise always—even after you have ceased to be a boy—and God help you to do it.

Your friend,

Baden Powell of Gilwell